This was an [...] months before [...] a little less than a year before he died. He was in the middle of the Down Grade Controversy. And though he couldn't have known this would be the last time he would address his beloved students in the Pastors College, the clarity and power of the themes – the reliability and power of the Bible, the certain success of the church, the power of the Holy Spirit – were timely then, and they seem just as timely today.

MARK DEVER,
Pastor, Capitol Hill Baptist Church, President, 9Marks
Washington, DC

No writing of C H Spurgeon should require commendation. However, each new generation of Christians needs an appropriate introduction, and this sparkling and startling address certainly fits the bill. How desperately we miss preaching like this today, amidst all the complacency, compromise and cowardice characteristic of so much professing evangelicalism. Here is perhaps the most rousing call to gospel arms you will ever encounter. If you can read it without being profoundly stirred, I strongly suggest you seek urgent spiritual help.

JONATHAN STEPHEN,
Principal, Wales Evangelical School of Theology, Bridgend, Wales

Nobody says it quite like Spurgeon. And Spurgeon in full flow, facing the critical issue of his day, is an impressive example of a heart burning with, and for, the glory of God. We have much to learn, and Spurgeon has much to teach us. This is a an excellent place to begin.

STEVE TIMMIS,
Director of Acts 29 Network in Western Europe

*The Greatest Fight in the World* by Charles Spurgeon, like William Gurnall's, *The Christian in Complete Armor* is not so much an example of expository preaching but a vivid and Biblical body of divinity describing the Gospel saturated life of the church in general and the Christian in particular who desires to serve Christ faithfully 'in the world' but not be 'of the world'. Christian Focus has, once again, provided for us another asset to fulfill our Savior's Great Commission – '…to make disciples…'

HARRY REEDER,
Pastor of Preaching & Leadership,
Briarwood Presbyterian Church, Birmingham, Alabama

This volume was to Spurgeon's students what 2 Timothy was to Timothy, a final installment of pastoral wisdom. Here, the Prince of Preachers bears his soul with instruction and inspiration for a new generation to take up the fight for personal holiness, passionate evangelism, and doctrinal fidelity. Always a wordsmith, Mr. Spurgeon leverages the power of language in this volume for spiritual motivation like nowhere else. I couldn't help reading it in one sitting.

RICK HOLLAND,
Senior Pastor,
Mission Road Bible Church, Kansas City, Kansas

There was a mouse who gathered around a number of mice and said to them, "Let me commend to you an elephant. What seems a tree trunk on our right is actually one of his legs and he has three others just like this. His nose from top to bottom is as long as thirty mice end to end. His skin is so tough that we'd break our teeth trying to gnaw it. When he makes a noise it shatters your ear drums. He is so tall I cannot see the top of his head. So be aware of this extraordinary being; be respectful and get out of his way when he walks by because we are so tiny he won't notice us. But he will never knowingly hurt us. He feeds on grass and leaves. He is benign and good. This is the elephant, the king of the jungle.

So it is when any preacher today is asked to commend a book of Charles Haddon Spurgeon's. A mouse is going to commend an elephant. We will add nothing at all to his reputation. He is simply utterly immense in his preaching, his energy, the size of his heart, his generosity and humour, his love for God, his discernment and wisdom. Read anything of his, and these addresses towards the end of his life are as good a place to begin to learn about one of God's true giants as any of his writing, and never stop reading him.

GEOFF THOMAS,
Minister, Alfred Place Baptist Church, Aberystwyth, Wales

# The Greatest Fight in the World

## The Final Manifesto

*C.H. Spurgeon*

CHRISTIAN
**HERITAGE**

Look out for *Living by Revealed Truth* by Tom Nettles (ISBN 978-1-78191-122-8). He has spent more than 15 years working on this magesterial biography of Charles Haddon Spurgeon which covers his life, ministry and also provides an indepth survey of his theology.

All Scripture is taken from the *King James Version*. All rights reserved.

Copyright © CH Spurgeon 2014

paperback ISBN 978-1-78191-329-1
epub ISBN 978-1-78191-348-2
Mobi ISBN 978-1-78191-349-9

Published in 2014
by
Christian Focus Publications, Ltd.
Geanies House, Fearn, Ross-shire,
IV20 1TW, Scotland, United Kingdom.
www.christianfocus.com

Cover design by Daniel van Straaten

Printed by Nørhaven, Denmark

# CONTENTS

# Foreword

<small>◆━━━━━━◆</small>

# Curtius Leaping:

*A Later Generation's Debt to Spurgeon*

Charles Spurgeon died on January 31, 1892, in the fifty-eighth year of his age. Forty-two of these years were spent in full time Christian ministry as a preacher of the gospel. Thirty-eight of them were spent under intense microscopic investigation by denominational pundits of all sorts. Some considered him shameful, a mountebank of the pulpit. Others saw him as supernaturally endowed with gifts and courage to halt the flood of infidelity and cure the slow ooze of religious insipidity overtaking English Christianity. The secular press, seemingly intent on decimating him by

9

riddling his public persona with a constant barrage of verbal rabbit-shot, could always find fodder for a good story by sneaking in a reporter to a Spurgeon sermon. In the end, his own denomination pushed him along the path of declining physical strength and emotional exuberance to a friendly grave. The Downgrade Controversy joined hands with gout and nephritis to aggravate the physical condition of Spurgeon culminating in his death in Mentone, France, where he had gone, as in so many years before, to reconstitute to continue the battle, a battle that he considered *The Greatest Fight in the World*.

Spurgeon raised the issue of theological defection in a series of articles in *The Sword and the Trowel* in 1887. This led to an outcry of protest from Baptist Union leaders who demanded that he particularize his charges so as not to cast a shadow over the entire denomination. Among those protesting were men that knew his charges were true and could themselves point to these instances of departure, both toward others and toward themselves. This disingenuous response convinced Spurgeon that he had delayed too long to sever this confederacy with evil. He resigned from the Baptist Union in October

1887, received a 'censure' from the Union Council early in 1888 for bringing up the issue of theological defection in the Union without providing supportive evidence, and saw the hope of reformation go down in flames in April 1888 with the Union's acceptance of a notoriously ambiguous confession of faith by a vote of 2000 to 7.

About the censure Spurgeon noted that 'the man [Spurgeon] with whom they professed to deliberate' in 'truth, and love, and good works,' they finally 'questioned and condemned.' He queried as to whether this resolution of the Council represented 'the opinion of the Baptist Union.' His own answer was 'I do not believe it.' Upon the Council's resolution, Spurgeon commented, 'It is quite as well that their resolution should be as incomprehensible as their doctrinal position is indefinable.' This turn of events should make none imagine that Spurgeon would 'cease from my protests against false doctrine or lay down the sword of which I have thrown away the scabbard.' He also resolved that he would not 'cease to expose doctrinal declension wherever I see it. With the Baptist Union as such I have now no hampering connection; but so far as it takes its part in the common departure from the truth, it will have to put up with my strictures, although it has so graciously kicked me under pretext of deliberation.'

A 'baseless Union' Spurgeon called the Baptist organization. His censure had come because Spurgeon sought to deal with error in an abstract form, (without naming the offenders) but he also plead for solidifying the Union with a confessional basis that would express the old evangelical faith. Spurgeon declared himself to be 'unable to sympathize with a man who says he has no creed.' At that time, as opposed to more robust former days, the only doctrinal affirmation of the Baptist Union was a common belief in the baptism of believers by immersion. In the climate created by an aggressive movement of 'Advanced Theology,' Spurgeon found this to be as disturbing as it was absurd.

How can we unite except upon some great common truths? And the doctrine of baptism by immersion is not sufficient for a groundwork. Surely, to be a Baptist is not everything. If I disagree with a man on ninety-nine points, but happen to be one with him in baptism, this can never furnish such ground of unity as I have with another with whom I believe in ninety-nine points, and only happen to differ upon one ordinance. To form a union with a single Scriptural ordinance as its sole distinctive reason for existence has been well likened to erecting a pyramid upon its apex: The whole edifice must sooner or later come down. I am not slow to avow my conviction that the immersions of believers is the baptism of Holy Scripture, but there are other truths beside this; and I cannot feel fellowship with a man because of this, if in other matters he is false to the teachings of Holy Scripture.[1]

He had found that his opponents, however, learned to use language 'rather to conceal a purpose than to express it,' and so he doubted 'whether any form of doctrine can be so worded as to be of the slightest use.'[2] This suspicion soon would be verified. Completely surprising to him, urged on by Spurgeon's friends in the Union, the council decided to recommend a confession in the April meeting, 1888. The outcome merely added to Spurgeon's distress. The art of subtle equivocation seemingly saved the unity

---

1. *The Sword and the Trowel,* February 1888, 83.
2. Ibid., 84, 82.

of the Union, but Spurgeon saw through it. His brother James had voted for the short confession thinking it was a vindication of Spurgeon, who responded, 'My brother made it clear that he was acting solely on his own account. The time was up, and he must decide without consulting anyone; he did so without compromising me, or anyone else. Of course I would ten thousand times rather go with him than differ from him; and in differing from him, I do only that which involves no disagreement of heart; we are equally earnest for the selfsame thing.'[3] His consternation increased when he found its meager assertions unobjectionable to the simple faithful but surrounded with a context and subtleties that would solve nothing. He was forced to read it 'in light of remarks made at the Council' (to which he had been made privy), his personal experience with some of its writers, and an encumbering footnote that greatly expanded the possible interpretations of some pivotal language. He observed, therefore, that 'I am not convinced that we have a real peace before us, or that we can ever arrive at a successful blending

---

3.    *The Sword and the Trowel,* May 1888, 1, 2.

of two parties which so greatly differ from each other.'[4]

In this same year, 1888, the doctrinal turmoil forced Spurgeon to restructure the basis of his own Pastors' College Conference. From within the body of his alumni, toleration toward the doctrinal positions that Spurgeon viewed as deadly to true Christianity had seeped and infected some of the prominent participants in that conference. 'The evil leaven,' he wrote 'has affected some few of them who were educated in our College.'[5] The attempt to remove them from the association uncovered other sympathizers, a group of one hundred that signed 'a mild protest' against Spurgeon's attempt at creating clarity and certainty of the theological basis for the conference. Instead of the unanimously held consensus, the split among his own men inflicted 'the sorest wound of all.' C. A. Davis, a leader of the opposition party, received an imploring letter from Spurgeon on 18 February 1888 explaining that his attempt at protest would be a 'purposeless conflict' and that Spurgeon had had 'all I can bear of bitterness.' Spurgeon explained his

---

4.   *The Sword and the Trowel,* May 1888, 2.
5.   *The Sword and the Trowel,* March 1888, 148.

procedure. He resigned his office as President of the Conference, dissolved the Conference, and reformed it on the more fulsome doctrinal basis. A 'Yes' vote approving the procedure would also be an approval of the 'basis' for the conference. This would be strictly enforced in forming the new conference. Davis's procedure opposing this, according to Spurgeon, 'has caused me the utmost grief, and forced me to this decision.'[6] He did not wonder that some might suspect his motives as well as his procedure for so much dust had been thrown in the air that even the eyes of an archangel would become bleary. Nevertheless, he had hopes for clearing the air. After most participants had sent in their votes, Spurgeon wrote the entire body.

> It is no small solace that nearly four hundred have voted yes right straight; and it will be a still greater joy, if, after the explanation given, many of you will do the like. By your love to me, I beseech you do nothing which would be half-hearted. We can do each other more good apart in open-hearted honesty than together with suppressed ill-will. It has been my joy to serve you, and I hope it will still be my privilege; but we can only work together

6.   G. Holden Pike, *The Life and Work of Charles Haddon Spurgeon* 6 vols (London: Cassell and Company, nd.) 6:298.

on the lines of the old Gospel, and if any of you are in love with 'advanced thought,' why do you wish to stay with such an old fogey as I am? Go your way and leave me an immovable old man, possibly the proper object of your pity, but assuredly not of your enmity, for I have striven to benefit you all according to my light and capacity. May the grace of our Lord be with the faithful among you, leading you to be wholly and boldly on the Lord's side in this day when men cannot endure sound doctrine! Yours heartily but with much sorrow, mingled with hopeful love,

C. H. Spurgeon

The final vote was 432 out of 496 for the new basis. Some of the 'nays' continued their protest against his procedure while others threatened 'to force themselves into our assembly, though they have departed from the faith that we hold.'[7] He felt encouraged, however, that those that remained would 'march on with all the greater and clearer confidence in God.' He wanted the College and its men to provide a 'great breakwater, firmly resisting the incoming flood of falsehood.'[8] While

---

7. *The Sword and the Trowel*, March 1888, 149, 150.
8. Ibid., 148.

renewing the conference, he would bring out some proven weapons for this fight.

In the midst of all this doctrinal tension, Spurgeon rushed into publication an edition of Louis Gaussen's *Theopneustia*. He looked closely at the problem in the Union and the College Conference and, as had been argued in the 'Downgrade' articles, believed intensely it began with questioning the divine inspiration of Scripture. In some remarks on 'Inspiration' Spurgeon noted that the pivotal issue in the battles between confessional orthodoxy and 'Advanced Theology' resides precisely in the 'true and real inspiration of the Holy Scriptures.' Spurgeon evoked strategic military images in calling the conflict the 'Thermopylae of Christendom.' He asserted, 'If we have in the Word of God no infallible standard of truth, we are at sea without a compass.' That dangerous journey should prompt us to 'part company altogether with the errorist, who overrides prophets and apostles, and practically regards his own inspiration as superior to theirs.' He had seen the tactic in history and felt it in the barbs aimed at him in the present.

The approved method of the present carnival of unbelief is not to reject the Bible altogether, but to raise doubts as to portions of it, and questions as to the uniform inspiration of it as a whole. Those who accept the Scriptures as infallible are sneered at as guilty of 'Bibliolatry', though they would to a man declare that they do not worship the book, but adore its author.[9]

So near both in time and in cause, Gaussen's book seemed fitting. Its author had been a part of a substantial revival of theology and adherence to the inerrancy of Scripture among the Reformed theologians of France in the first half of the nineteenth century. Spurgeon saw the dynamic and the issues with which he was battling in the present moment to be 'so sadly similar to that which prevailed in Geneva fifty years ago,' that he 'reissued it in the earnest hope that it may establish the wavering and win back the wandering.'[10] Spurgeon sought to sow new seed while he conserved the fruit of past seed-times.

The conservation project resulted in his newly formed 'Pastors' College Evangelical Association.' Spurgeon addressed them on April 17, 1888, almost one week before

---

9.    'Remarks on Inspiration,' *The Sword and the Trowel,* May 1888, 207.
10.   *The Sword and the Trowel,* June 1888, 270.

the Baptist Union vote on the Confession.
Reflecting on how difficult it had become
in a time of such intense excitement to avoid
offending even when measuring one's words
with great care, Spurgeon observed, 'Certainly
my criticisms have cost me more pain than
they have inflicted.'[11] Steering clear of
personalities, but focusing on issues, Spurgeon
talked about the 'Evils of the Present Time.'
In his own engaging way, he spoke of the
attack on fundamental truth such as scriptural
authority and justification by faith. He pointed
to the misrepresentations and distortions of
truth such as the wrath to come. In light of
the immediately upcoming meeting of the
Baptist Union, Spurgeon also noted the evil
of delay in 'decision for the truth among truly
good men.' These brethren in the Lord Jesus
cannot make up their mind to separate from
error. Spurgeon encouraged his men to be
willing to be abused and ridiculed rather than
be false to the Lord. An 'insatiable craving for
amusements' was another evil of the times.
'Within suitable bounds,' Spurgeon allowed,
'recreation is necessary and profitable; but it
never was the business of the Christian church

---

11.   Ibid., 258.

to supply the world with amusements.'[12] Neither 'Musical Chairs,' nor 'Punch and Judy' shows are warranted venues of worship. With such shenanigans present, none should wonder that another evil lies in 'the lack of intense piety in many of the Churches.' The lack of family worship, the neglect of prayer meetings, and the preferred attendance upon public dinners and sing-songs reveals the god served by many church members and active ministers of superficial, if any at all, commitment to godliness. One error breeds another and then the two feed off of each other. So absent piety creates a lack of desire for godly ministers and such ministers make piety decline even further. Church members seem indifferent as to the personal piety of the preacher but are insistent that he be clever. Content of proclamation is of minor importance if he can draw a crowd, or please the *elite*. 'One would think they were looking for a conjuror rather than a pastor.' Indifferent to truth and overlooking error, they glow with admiration 'so long as he can talk glibly and keep up a reputation as a speaker.'[13]

12. *The Sword and the Trowel,* June 1888, 262.
13. *The Sword and the Trowel,* June 1888, 263.

Spurgeon found society in general to be less oriented to deal seriously with spiritual things. Two phenomena from divergent sources contributed to this. One, many evangelicals forsook sober teaching for 'pandering to sensationalism' in worship. 'Like dram-drinking the thirst for excitement grows.' Two, the celebration of doubt on the part of ministers had created a general capitulation to infidelity. 'The ministers have done it. They preached the people out of their faith in the Scriptures; they taught them to be doubters. The most mischievous minister of Satan that I know of is the minister of the gospel, who not only doubts the truth in his own soul, but propagates doubt in the minds of others by his criticisms, innuendos, and triflings with words.' Spurgeon considered it a kind of willful murder to 'expel the soul from pious phrases and still use them.' He felt viscerally the absurdity of ministers who 'prefer the chase after truth to truth itself' and feel satisfied that their prey 'should perpetually escape him.'[14] He reminded the reconstituted conference that their 'chief end is to glorify God.' The first business is not to 'convert sinners nor to

---

14.  *The Sword and the Trowel*, July 1888, 340

edify the saints, but to glorify God.' If they preach truly and none are converted they still are a sweet savour of Christ unto God. 'The sacrifice of Jesus is that which makes the world bearable to a holy God, and the preaching of that sacrifice is a savour of rest unto him.' Even in rough times they must remember that they are fishermen, not the sailors of yachts. They must ever strive to be better men, not be content by consoling themselves that someone else's work is worse than theirs. It is a strange and perverse attempt at comfort to be told that someone else is in even greater misery. They must be more loving so as to be more earnest in seeking to rescue sinners from the wrath to come. Though they lived in perpetual sacrifice pecuniarily, they must yet be intent on not resting in such a high calling, not being loiterers but laborers. To the sacrifice of earthly comfort they must add the sacrifice of peer approval: 'In the battle for the truth let your personal comfort and reputation go to the winds.'[15] To the peculiar demands of their unique ministries they must give themselves and build their people upon everlasting and imperishable realities. 'I fear,' Spurgeon noted,

---

15.   *The Sword and the Trowel,* July 1888, 341.

' the ideas of the ministry with some men is as much on the down-grade as their doctrine.'[16] Attention to fundamental truths among their hearers must be a priority. Accordingly, they must look distinctly to 'labor distinctly for the immediate salvation of your hearers.' As the necessary outflow of this Spurgeon urged, 'Let us inculcate with all our might the practice of holiness,' which he called the 'visible side of salvation.' If evangelism should assume a pursuit of holiness, then, if the love the Lord and value men's souls, each should 'be careful about the admission of members into the church.' This includes the particular stewardship of 'separation from those who would be likely to injure your spiritual life.' Spurgeon declared that he would 'no more associate with one who denied the faith than with a drunkard or a thief.' One must guard his spirituals as well as his morals. Thinking of this in terms of the recent reorganization of the Conference, Spurgeon added, 'we must bind ourselves more closely, and seek to render help to each other and to all who are of the same mind in the Lord.'[17] Again, reflecting on

---

16.  Ibid., 341.
17.  *The Sword and the Trowel*, July 1888, 343.

the importance of vital truth as higher than denominational loyalty, Spurgeon reinforced this point.

Denominational divisions sink in the presence of the truth of God. To my mind, the grand distinction to be now observed is found in evangelical doctrine, of which our Lord's substitutionary sacrifice is the centre and the soul. Where we see faithful brethren struggling, we ought to lay ourselves out to help them, for they are sure to be the objects of inveterate opposition. Lovers of the old faith should stand shoulder to shoulder, to remove the injustice of the past, and frustrate the opposition of the future.[18]

As Spurgeon closed this initial message to the doctrinally invigorated Pastors' College Conference, he reminded them that times of decline and opposition had come before, but that God would protect and revive his truth. To that end they must be men of prayer. 'Prayer is the master weapon.' Not all could argue, but all could pray; not all could be leaders, but all could be pleaders; not all could be mighty in rhetoric, but all could be persistent in prayer. It is better to be

18.   *The Sword and the Trowel*, July 1888, 344.

eloquent with God than with men. 'Prayer links us with the Eternal, the Omnipotent, the Infinite, and hence it is our chief resort.'[19]

The oppressive disappointment concentrated in so few months had given Spurgeon resolve to set before his men, newly pledged to faithfulness, all that he felt was important for a ministerial stewardship well executed. Doctrinal orthodoxy and honesty, personal holiness, zeal for the church and its purity, earnestness for the souls of sinners, and attention to the disciplines of personal devotion to Christ must be the harmoniously blended elements of a gospel preacher.

In the year 1891, Spurgeon would finish all that he would do both for the Metropolitan Tabernacle, for the Pastor' College, and for the Pastors' College Conference. He began *The Sword and the Trowel* that year with an article entitled 'The Present Crisis.' It is a jeremiad overladen with a sense of having been defeated for the moment, bloodied, but finally unbowed, and confident that truth will rebound to take a firmer grasp on the people of God than ever. Having surveyed the amazing compromises in every sphere

19.  Ibid., 345.

of society, Spurgeon sighed, 'Religion itself, weary of laborious advance, regards her holy scruples as *impedimenta* and adopts the methods of the world, while her doctrinal teaching is left, like some ancient Caesar's camp, to be viewed as a curiosity by this advanced generation.'[20] Opposition, though shallow, haughty, dismissive, and ephemeral carries a brazen confidence that the old faith can be dealt with by a mere sneer. 'Certain of us,' Spurgeon confessed, 'are distressed beyond measure by that which others enter upon with a light heart.'[21] These tactics appear, for the moment, to carry the day. 'New teachings and new methods mar the peace of churches which, for many generations, have held to the once-delivered faith. The intrusion has been wanton and illegal; but what of that? Protests are of no avail; it usually suffices to answer them with a sneer. Where contempt would scarcely be prudent, the pretence of agreement is made to cover over a fatal difference, and to give opportunity to stab the truth in the back.'[22] Spurgeon, however,

---

20. *The Sword and the Trowel,* January 1891, 1.
21. *The Sword and the Trowel,* January 1891, 2.
22. Ibid., 2.

even in the bleakest moment maintained and expressed his confidence in the inviolable resilience of divinely revealed truth and in God's purpose to establish it in the hearts of his people. 'When those who rule the hour,' Spurgeon reflected, 'are no longer able to silence the much-enduring people, there will be a return to the former beliefs, and this will be accompanied by a firmer adhesion to them in the future.' Could this be the generation in which Spurgeon's vision takes on solid flesh and blood?

Spurgeon ended the article on 'The Present Crisis' with the challenge, 'There is a faith which turns to flight the armies of the aliens. May we each one possess it now.'[23] The message in this booklet, preached in 1891 at the final Pastors' College Conference that Spurgeon attended, sought to concentrate his peroration into three essential convictions of Christian ministry—the irreducible context in which this greatest fight—putting to flight the armies of the aliens—must be fought. First was the armory, the authoritative and only effectual weapon in this battle, the Holy Scripture. Second, he discussed the

---

23.    *The Sword and the Trowel,* January 1891, 3.

army, that body that a minister must prepare for enduring and courageous conflict, the church. Third, Spurgeon looked at the source of power from which soldiers of truth must fully and confidently draw fresh strength and courage and to which they must look for the final victory, the Holy Spirit. With these admonitions considered in a variety of parts, Spurgeon shouts, 'Welcome to the Greatest Fight in the World.'

*Tom Nettles*
*October 2013*

# Introduction

*Fight the good fight of faith.*
1 Timothy 6:12

May all the prayers which have already been offered up be answered abundantly and speedily! May more of such pleading follow that in which we have united! The most memorable part of past Conferences has been the holy concert of believing prayer; and I trust we are not falling off in that respect, but growing yet more fervent and prevalent in intercession. On his knees the believer is invincible.

I am greatly concerned about this Address for many months before it comes on: assuredly it is to me the child of many prayers. I should like to be able to speak well on so worthy an occasion, wherein the best of speech may well be enlisted; but I desire to be, as our brother's prayer has put it, absolutely in the Lord's hands, in this matter as well as in every other. I would be willing to speak with stammering tongue if God's purpose could so be answered more fully; and I would even gladly lose all power of speech if, by being famished as to human words, you might feed the better on that spiritual meat which is to be found alone in Him, who is the incarnate Word of God.

I may say to you, as speakers, that I am persuaded we should prepare ourselves with diligence, and try to do our very best in our great Master's service. I think I have read that when a handful of lion-like Greeks held the pass against the Persians, a spy, who came to see what they were doing, went back and told the great king that they were poor creatures, for they were busied in combing their hair. The despot saw things in a true light when he learned that a people who could adjust their hair before battle had set a great value on their heads, and would not bow them to a coward's death. If we are very careful to use our best language when proclaiming eternal truths, we may leave our opponents to infer that we are still more careful of the doctrines themselves. We must not be untidy soldiers when a great fight is before us, for that would look like despondency. Into the battle against false doctrine, and worldliness, and sin, we advance without a fear as to the ultimate issue; and therefore our talk should not be that of ragged passion, but of well-considered principle. It is not ours to be slovenly, since we look to be triumphant. Do your work well at this time, that all men may see that you are not going to be driven from it.

The Persian said, when on another occasion he saw a handful of warriors advancing, 'That little handful of men! Surely, they cannot mean fighting!' But one who stood by said, 'Yes, they do, for they have burnished their shields, and brightened their armour.' Men mean business, depend upon it, when they are not to be hurried into disorder. It was the way amongst the Greeks, when they had a bloody day before them, to show the stern joy of warriors by being well adorned. I think, brethren, that when we have great work to do for Christ, and mean doing it, we shall not go to the pulpit or the platform to say the first thing that comes to the lip. If we speak for Jesus we ought to speak at our best, though, even then, men are not killed by the glitter of shields, nor by the smoothness of a warrior's hair; but a higher power is needed to cut through coats of mail. To the God of armies I look up. May He defend the right! But with no careless step do I advance to the front; neither does any doubt possess me. We are feeble, but the Lord our God is mighty, and the battle is the Lord's, rather than ours.

Only one fear is upon me to a certain degree. I am anxious that my deep sense of responsibility may not lessen my efficiency. A man may feel that he ought to do so well that, for that very reason, he may not do as well as he might. An overpowering feeling of responsibility may breed paralysis. I once recommended a young clerk to a bank, and his friends very properly gave him strict charge to be very careful in his figures. This advice he heard times out of mind. He became so extremely careful as to grow nervous, and whereas he had been accurate before, his anxiety caused him to make blunder after blunder, till he left his situation.

It is possible to be so anxious as to how and what you shall speak, that your manner grows constrained, and you forget those very points which you meant to make most prominent.

Brethren, I am telling some of my private thoughts to you, because we are alike in our calling; and having the same experiences, it does us good to know that it is so. We who lead have the same weaknesses and troubles as you who follow. We must prepare, but we must also trust in Him without whom nothing begins, continues, or ends aright.

I have this comfort, that even if I should not speak adequately upon my theme, the topic itself will speak to you. There is something even in starting an appropriate subject. If a man speaks well upon a subject which has no practical importance, it is not well that he should have spoken. As one of the ancients said, 'It is idle to speak much to the point upon a matter which itself is not to the point.' Carve a cherry-stone with the utmost skill, and at best it is but a cherry-stone; while a diamond if badly cut is still a precious stone. If the matter be of great weight, even if the man cannot speak up to his theme, yet to call attention to it is no vain thing. The subjects which we shall consider at this time ought to be considered, and to be considered just now. I have chosen present and pressing truths, and if you will think them out for yourselves, you will not lose the time occupied by this address. With what inward fervour do I pray that we may all be profited by this hour of meditation!

Happily the themes are such that I can exemplify them even in this address. As a smith can teach his apprentice *while* making a horseshoe; yes, and *by* making a horseshoe; so can we make our own sermons examples of the doctrine they contain. In this case we can practise what we preach, if the Lord be with us. A lecturer in cookery instructs his pupils by following his own recipes. He prepares a dish before his audience, and while he describes the viands and their preparation, he tastes the food himself, and his friends are refreshed also. He will succeed by his dainty dishes, even if he is not a man of eloquent speech. The man who feeds is surer of success than he who only plays well upon an instrument, and leaves with his audience no memory but that of pleasant sound. If the subjects which we bring before our people are in themselves good, they will make up for our want of skill in setting them forth. So long as the guests get the spiritual meat, the servitor at the table may be happy to be forgotten.

*My topics have to do with our life-work, with the crusade against error and sin in which we are engaged.* I hope that every man here wears the red cross on his heart, and is pledged to do and dare for Christ and for His cross, and never to be satisfied till Christ's foes are routed and Christ Himself is satisfied. Our fathers used to speak of 'The Cause of God and Truth'; and it is for this that we bear arms, the few against the many, the feeble against the mighty. Oh, to be found good soldiers of Jesus Christ!

Three things are of the utmost importance just now, and, indeed, they always have stood, and always will stand in the front rank for practical purposes. The first is *our armoury,* which is the inspired Word; the second is *our army,* the church of the living God, called out by Himself, which we must lead under our Lord's command; and the third is *our strength,* by which we wear the armour and wield the sword. The Holy

Spirit is our power to be and to do; to suffer and to serve; to grow and to fight; to wrestle and to overcome. Our third theme is of main importance, and though we place it last, we rank it first.

# 1

## Our Armoury

We will begin with **our armoury**. That armoury is to me, at any rate—and I hope it is to each one of you—**the Bible**. To us Holy Scripture is as 'the tower of David builded for an armoury, whereon there hang a thousand bucklers, all shields of mighty men.'[1] If we want weapons we must come here for them, and here only. Whether we seek the sword of offence or the shield of defence, we must find it within the volume of inspiration. If others have any other storehouse, I confess

---

1. Song of Solomon 4:4.

39

at once I have none. I have nothing else to preach when I have got through with this book. Indeed, I can have no wish to preach at all if I may not continue to expound the subjects which I find in these pages. What else is worth preaching? Brethren, the truth of God is the only treasure for which we seek, and the Scripture is the only field in which we dig for it.

*We need nothing more than God has seen fit to reveal.* Certain errant spirits are never at home till they are abroad: they crave for a something which I think they will never find, either in heaven above, or in the earth beneath, or in the water under the earth, so long as they are in their present mind. They never rest, for they will have nothing to do with an infallible revelation; and hence they are doomed to wander throughout time and eternity, and find no abiding city. For the moment they glory as if they were satisfied with their last new toy; but in a few months it is sport to them to break in pieces all the notions which they formerly prepared with care, and paraded with delight. They go up a hill only to come down again. Indeed, they say that the pursuit of truth is better than truth itself. They like fishing better than the fish; which may very well be true, since their fish are very small, and very full of bones. These men are as great at destroying their own theories as certain paupers are at tearing up their clothes. They begin again *de novo,* times without number: their house is always having its foundation digged out. They should be good at beginnings; for they have always been beginning since we have known them. They are as the rolling thing before the whirlwind, or 'like the troubled sea, when it cannot rest, whose waters cast up mire and dirt.'[2] Although their cloud is not that cloud which betokened the divine presence, yet it is always moving before them, and their tents are scarcely pitched before it is time for the stakes to be pulled up again. These men are not even seeking certainty; their heaven lies in shunning all fixed truth, and following every will-o'-the-wisp of speculation: they are ever learning, but they never come to the knowledge of the truth.

As for us, we cast anchor in the haven of the Word of God. Here is our peace, our strength, our life, our motive, our hope, our happiness. God's Word is our ultimatum.

2.    Isaiah 57:20.

Here we have it. Our understanding cries,
'I have found it'; our conscience asserts that
here is *the truth;* and our heart finds here
a support to which all her affections can
cling; and hence we rest content.

*If the revelation of God were not enough
for our faith, what could we add to it?* Who
can answer this question? What would any
man propose to add to the sacred Word?
A moment's thought would lead us to scout
with derision the most attractive words of
men, if it were proposed to add them to
the Word of God. The fabric would not be
of a piece. Would you add rags to a royal
vestment? Would you pile the filth of the
streets in a king's treasury? Would you join
the pebbles of the sea-shore to the diamonds
of Golconda? Anything more than the Word
of God sets before us, for us to believe and
to preach as the life of men, seems utterly
absurd to us; yet we confront a generation
of men who are always wanting to discover
a new motive power, and a new gospel for
their churches. The coverlet of their bed does
not seem to be long enough, and they would
fain borrow a yard or two of linsey-woolsey
from the Unitarian, the Agnostic, or even the

Atheist. Well; if there be any spiritual force or heavenward power to be found beyond that reported of in this Book, I think we can do without it: indeed, it must be such a sham that we are better without it. The Scriptures in their own sphere are like God in the universe—All-sufficient. In them is revealed all the light and power the mind of man can need in spiritual things. We hear of other motive power beyond that which lies in the Scriptures, but we believe such a force to be a pretentious nothing. A train is off the lines, or otherwise unable to proceed, and a break-down gang has arrived. Engines are brought to move the great impediment. At first there seems to be no stir: the engine power is not enough. Harken! A small boy has it. He cries, 'Father, if they have not power enough, I will lend them my rocking-horse to help them.' We have had the offer of a considerable number of rocking-horses of late. They have not accomplished much that I can see, but they promised fair. I fear their effect has been for evil rather than good: they have moved the people to derision, and have driven them out of the places of worship which once they were glad to crowd. The new toys have been exhibited, and the people, after seeing them for a little, have moved on to other toy-shops. These fine new nothings have done no good, and they never will do any good while the world standeth. The Word of God is quite sufficient to interest and bless the souls of men throughout all time; but novelties soon fail. 'Surely,' cries one, 'we must add our own thoughts thereto.' My brother, think by all means; but the thoughts of God are better than yours. You may shed fine thoughts, as trees in autumn cast their leaves; but there is One who knows more about your thoughts than you do, and He thinks little of them. Is it not written, 'The Lord knoweth the thoughts of man, that they are vanity'?[3] To liken *our* thoughts to the great thoughts of God, would be a gross absurdity. Would you bring your candle to show the sun? Your nothingness to replenish the eternal all? It is better to be silent before the Lord, than to dream of supplementing what He has spoken. The Word of the Lord is to the conceptions of men as a garden to a wilderness. Keep within the covers of the sacred book, and you are in the land which

---

3.    Psalm 94:11.

floweth with milk and honey; why seek to add to it the desert sands?

*Try not to cast anything forth from the perfect volume.* If you find it there, there let it stand, and be it yours to preach it according to the analogy and proportion of faith. That which is worthy of God's revealing is worthy of our preaching; and that is all too little for me to claim for it. 'By every word of the Lord doth man live.'[4] 'Every word of God is pure: he is a shield unto them that put their trust in him'[5] Let every revealed truth be brought forth in its own season. Go not elsewhere for a subject: with such infinity before you, there can be no need that you should do so; with such glorious truth to preach, it will be wanton wickedness if you do.

*The adaption of all this provision for our warfare we have already tested:* the weapons of our armoury are the very best; for we have made trial of them, and have found them so. Some of you, younger brethren, have only tested the Scripture a little as yet; but others of us, who are now getting grey, can assure you that we have tried the Word, as silver is

---

4.   Deuteronomy 8:3.
5.   Proverbs 30:5.

tried in a furnace of earth; and it has stood every test, even unto seventy times seven. The sacred Word has endured more criticism than the best accepted form of philosophy or science, and it has survived every ordeal. As a living divine has said, 'After its present assailants are all dead, their funeral sermons will be preached from this Book—not one verse omitted—from the first page of Genesis to the last page of Revelation.' Some of us have lived for many years, in daily conflict, perpetually putting to the proof the Word of God; and we can honestly give you this assurance, that it is equal to every emergency. After using this sword of two edges upon coats of mail, and bucklers of brass, we find no notch in its edge. It is neither broken nor blunted in the fray. It would cleave the devil himself, from the crown of his head to the sole of his foot; and yet it would show no sign of failure whatsoever. To-day it is still the self-same mighty Word of God that it was in the hands of our Lord Jesus. How it strengthens us when we remember the many conquests of souls which we have achieved through the sword of the Spirit! Have any of you known or heard of such a thing as conversion wrought by any other doctrine than that which is in the Word? I should like to have a catalogue of conversions wrought by modern theology. I would subscribe for a copy of such a work. I will not say what I might do with it after I had read it; but I would, at least, increase its sale by one copy, just to see what progressive divinity pretends to have done. Conversions through the doctrines of universal restitution! Conversions through the doctrines of doubtful inspiration! Conversions to the love of God, and to faith in his Christ, by hearing that the death of the Saviour was only the consummation of a grand example, but not a substitutionary sacrifice! Conversions by a gospel out of which all the gospel has been drained! They say, 'Wonders will never cease'; but such wonders will never begin. Let them report changes of heart so wrought, and give us an opportunity of testing them; and then, perchance, we may consider whether it is worth our while to leave that Word which we have tried in hundreds, and, some of us here, in many thousands of cases, and have always found effectual for salvation. We know why they sneer at conversions. These are grapes which such foxes cannot reach, and therefore they are sour. As we believe in the new birth, and expect to see it in thousands of cases, we shall adhere to that Word of truth by which the Holy Spirit works regeneration. In a word, in our warfare we shall keep to the old weapon of the sword of the Spirit, until we can find a better. 'There is none like that; give it me', is at present our verdict.

How often we have seen the Word made effectual for consolation! It is, as one brother expressed it in prayer, a difficult thing to deal with broken hearts. What a fool I have felt myself to be when trying to bring forth a prisoner out of Giant Despair's Castle! How hard it is to persuade despondency to hope! How have I tried to trap my game by every art known to me; but when almost in my grasp the creature has burrowed another hole! I had dug him out of twenty already, and then have had to begin again. The convicted sinner uses all kinds of arguments to prove that he cannot be saved. The inventions of despair are as many as the devices of self-confidence. There is no letting light into the dark cellar of doubt, except through the window of the Word of God. Within the Scripture there is a balm for every wound, a salve for every sore. Oh, the wondrous power in the Scripture to create a soul of hope within the ribs of despair, and bring eternal light into the darkness which has made a long midnight in the inmost soul! Often have we tried the Word of the Lord as 'the cup of consolation', and it has never failed to cheer the despondent. We know what we say, for we have witnessed the blessed facts: the Scriptures of truth, applied by the Holy Spirit, have brought peace and joy to those who sat in darkness and in the valley of the shadow of death.

We have also observed the excellence of the Word in the edification of believers, and in the production of righteousness, holiness, and usefulness. We are always being told, in these days, of the 'ethical' side of the gospel. I pity those to whom this is a novelty. Have they not discovered this before? We have always been dealing with the ethical side of the gospel; indeed, we find it ethical all over. There is no true doctrine which has not been fruitful in good works. Payson wisely said, 'If there is one fact, one doctrine, or promise in the Bible, which has produced no practical effect upon your temper or conduct, be assured that you do not truly believe it.' All Scriptural teaching has its practical purpose, and its practical result; and what we have to say, not as a matter of discovery, but as a matter of plain common sense, is this, that if we have had fewer fruits than we could wish *with* the tree, we suspect that there will be no fruit at all when the tree has gone, and the roots are dug up. The very root of holiness lies in the gospel of our Lord Jesus Christ; and if this be removed with a view to more fruitfulness, the most astounding folly will have been committed. We have seen a fine morality, a stern integrity, a delicate purity, and, what is more, a devout holiness, produced by the doctrines of grace. We see consecration in life, we see calm resignation in the hour of suffering, we see joyful confidence in the article of death, and these, not in a few instances, but as the general outcome of intelligent faith in the teachings of Scripture. We have even wondered at the sacred result of the old gospel. Though we are accustomed often-times to see it, it never loses its charm. We have seen poor men and women yielding themselves to Christ, and living for Him, in a way that has made our hearts to bow in adoration of the God of grace. We have said, 'This must be a true gospel which can produce such lives as these.' If we have not talked so much about ethics as some have done, we remember an old saying of the country folk: 'Go to such a place to hear about good works, but go to another place to see them.' Much talk, little work. Great cry is the token of little wool. Some have preached good works till there has scarcely been left a decent person in the parish; while others have preached free grace and dying love in such a way that sinners have become saints, and saints have been as boughs loaded down with fruit to the praise and glory of God. Having seen the harvest which springs from our seed, we are not going to change it at the dictates of this whimsical age.

Especially we have seen and tested the efficacy of the Word of God when we have been by the sick bed. I was, but a few days ago, by the side of one of our elders, who appeared to be dying; and it was like heaven below to converse with him. I never saw so much joy at a wedding as I saw in that quiet chamber. He hoped soon to be with Jesus; and he was joyful in the prospect. He said, 'I have no doubt, no cloud, no trouble, no want; nay,

I have not even a wish. The doctrine you have taught has served me to live by, and now it serves me to die by. I am resting upon the precious blood of Christ, and it is a firm foundation.' And he added, 'How silly all those letters against the gospel now appear to me! I have read some of them, and I have noted the attacks upon the old faith, but they seem quite absurd to me now that I lie on the verge of eternity. What could the new doctrine do for me now?' I came down from my interview greatly strengthened and gladdened by the good man's testimony; and all the more was I personally comforted because it was the Word which I myself had constantly preached which had been such a blessing to my friend. If God had so owned it from so poor an instrument, I felt that the Word itself must be good indeed. I am never so happy amidst all the shouts of youthful merriment as on the day when I hear the dying testimony of one who is resting on the everlasting gospel of the grace of God. The ultimate issue, as seen upon a dying-bed, is a true test, as it is an inevitable one. Preach that which will enable men to face death without fear, and you will preach nothing but the old gospel.

Brethren, we will array ourselves in that which God has supplied us in the armoury of inspired Scripture, because every weapon in it has been tried and proved in many ways; and never has any part of our panoply failed us.

Moreover, we shall evermore keep to the Word of God, because *we have had experience of its power within ourselves.* It is not so long ago that you will have forgotten how, like a hammer, the Word of God broke your flinty heart, and brought down your stubborn will. By the Word of the Lord you were brought to the cross, and comforted by the atonement. That Word breathed a new life into you; and when, for the first time, you knew yourself to be a child of God, you felt the ennobling power of the gospel received by faith. The Holy Spirit wrought your salvation through the Holy Scriptures. You trace your conversion, I am sure, to the Word of the Lord; for this alone is 'perfect, converting the soul.'[6] Whoever may have been the man who spoke it, or whatever may have been the book in which you read it, it was not man's Word, nor man's thought upon God's Word, but the Word itself, which made you know salvation in the Lord Jesus. It

---

6.    Psalm 19:7.

53

was neither human reasoning, nor the force of eloquence, nor the power of moral suasion, but the omnipotence of the Spirit, applying the Word itself, that gave you rest and peace and joy through believing. We are ourselves trophies of the power of the sword of the Spirit; He leads us in triumph in every place, the willing captives of His grace. Let no man marvel that we keep close to it.

How many times since conversion has Holy Scripture been everything to you! You have your fainting fits, I suppose: have you not been restored by the precious cordial of the promise of the Faithful One? A passage of Scripture laid home to the heart speedily quickens the feeble heart into mighty action. Men speak of waters that revive the spirits, and tonics that brace the constitution; but the Word of God has been more than this to us, times beyond count. Amidst temptations sharp and strong, and trials fierce and bitter, the Word of the Lord has preserved us. Amidst discouragements which damped our hopes, and disappointments which wounded our hearts, we have felt ourselves strong to do and bear, because the assurances of help which we find in our Bibles have brought us a secret, unconquerable energy.

Brethren, we have had experience of the elevation which the Word of God can give us—upliftings towards God and heaven. If you get studying books contrary to the inspired volume, are you not conscious of slipping downwards? I have known some to whom such reading has been as a mephitic vapour surrounding them with the death-damp. Yes; and I may add, that to forego your Bible reading for the perusal even of good books would soon bring a conscious descending of the soul. Have you not found that even gracious books may be to you as a plain to look down upon, rather than as a summit to which to aspire? You have come up to their level long ago, and get no higher by reading them: it is idle to spend precious time upon them. Was it ever so with you and the Book of God? Did you ever rise above its simplest teaching, and feel that it tended to draw you downward? Never! In proportion as your mind becomes saturated with Holy Scripture, you are conscious of being lifted right up, and carried aloft as on eagles' wings. You seldom come down from a solitary Bible reading without feeling that you have drawn near to God: I say a solitary one; for when reading with others, the danger is that stale comments may be flies in the pot of ointment. The prayerful study of the Word is not only a means of instruction, but an act of devotion wherein the transforming power of grace is often exercised, changing us into the image of Him of whom the Word is a mirror. Is there anything, after all, like the Word of God when the open book finds open hearts?

When I read the lives of such men as Baxter, Brainerd, McCheyne, and many others, why, I feel like one who has bathed himself in some cool brook after having gone a journey through a black country, which left him dusty and depressed; and this result comes of the fact that such men embodied Scripture in their lives and illustrated it in their experience. The washing of water by the Word is what they had, and what we need. We must get it where they found it. To see the effects of the truth of God in the lives of holy men is confirmatory to faith and stimulating to holy aspiration. Other influences do not help us to such a sublime ideal of consecration. If you read the Babylonian books of the present day, you will catch their spirit, and it is a foreign one, which will draw you aside from the Lord your God. You may also get great harm from divines in whom there is much pretence of the Jerusalem dialect, but their speech is half of Ashdod: these will confuse your mind and defile your faith. It may chance that a book which is upon the whole excellent, which has little taint about it, may do you more mischief than a thoroughly bad one. Be careful; for works of this kind come forth from the press like clouds of locusts. Scarcely can you find in these days a book which is quite free from the modern leaven, and the least particle of it ferments till it produces the wildest error. In reading books of the new order, though no palpable falsehood may appear, you are conscious of a twist being given you, and of a sinking in the tone of your spirit; therefore be on your guard. But with your Bible you may always feel at ease; there every breath from every quarter brings life and health. If you keep close to the inspired book, you can suffer no harm; say rather you are at the fountain-head of all moral and spiritual good. This is fit food for men of God: this is the bread which nourishes the highest life.

After preaching the gospel for forty years, and after printing the sermons I have preached for more than six-and-thirty years, reaching now to the number of 2,200 in weekly succession, I am fairly entitled to speak about the fulness and richness of the Bible, as a preacher's book. Brethren, it is inexhaustible. No question about freshness will arise if we keep closely to the text of the sacred volume. There can be no difficulty as to finding themes totally distinct from those we have handled before; the variety is as infinite as the fulness. A long life will only suffice us to skirt the shores of this great continent of light. In the forty years of my own ministry I have only touched the hem of the garment of divine truth; but what virtue has flowed out of it! The Word is like its Author, infinite, immeasurable, without end. If you were ordained to be a preacher throughout eternity, you would have before you a theme equal to everlasting demands. Brothers, shall we each have a pulpit somewhere amidst the spheres? Shall we have a parish of millions of leagues? Shall we have voices so strengthened as to reach attentive constellations? Shall we be witnesses for the Lord of grace to

myriads of worlds which will be wonder-
struck when they hear of the incarnate God?
Shall we be surrounded by pure intelligences
enquiring and searching into the mystery of
God manifest in the flesh? Will the unfallen
worlds desire to be instructed in the glorious
gospel of the blessed God?[7] And will each
one of us have his own tale to tell of our
experience of infinite love? I think so, since
the Lord has saved us 'to the intent that now
unto the principalities and powers in heavenly
places might be known by the church of the
manifold wisdom of God.' If such be the
case, our Bibles will suffice for ages to come
for new themes every morning, and for fresh
songs and discourses world without end.

We are resolved, then, since we have this
arsenal supplied for us of the Lord, and since
we want no other, to use the Word of God
only, and *to use it with greater energy. We are
resolved*—and I hope there is no dissentient
among us—*to know our Bibles better.* Do we
know the sacred volume half so well as we
should know it? Have we laboured after as
complete a knowledge of the Word of God
as many a critic has obtained of his favourite

---

7.    Ephesians 3:10.

classic? Is it not possible that we still meet with passages of Scripture which are new to us? Should it be so? Is there any part of what the Lord has written which you have never read? I was struck with my brother Archibald Brown's observation, that he bethought himself that unless he read the Scriptures through from end to end there might be inspired teachings which had never been known to him, and so he resolved to read the books in their order; and having done so once, he continued the habit. Have we, any of us, omitted to do this? Let us begin at once. I love to see how readily certain of our brethren turn up an appropriate passage, and then quote its fellow, and crown all with a third. They seem to know exactly the passage which strikes the nail on the head. They have their Bibles, not only in their hearts, but at their fingers' ends. This is a most valuable attainment for a minister. A good textuary is a good theologian. Certain others, whom I esteem for other things, are yet weak on this point, and seldom quote a text of Scripture correctly: indeed, their alterations jar on the ear of the Bible reader. It is sadly common among ministers to add a word or subtract a word from the passage, or in some way to debase the language of sacred writ. How often have I heard brethren speak about making 'your calling and salvation' sure! Possibly they hardly enjoyed so much as we do the Calvinistic word 'election', and therefore they allowed the meaning; nay, in some cases contradict it. Our reverence for the great Author of Scripture should forbid all mauling of His words. No alteration of Scripture can by any possibility be an improvement. Believers in verbal inspiration should be studiously careful to be verbally correct. The gentlemen who see errors in Scripture may think themselves competent to amend the language of the Lord of hosts; but we who believe God, and accept the very words He uses, may not make so presumptuous an attempt. Let us quote the words as they stand in the best possible translation, and it will be better still if we know the original, and can tell if our version fails to give the sense. How much mischief may arise out of an accidental alteration of the Word! Blessed are they who are in accord with the divine teaching, and receive its true meaning, as the Holy Ghost teaches them!

Oh, that we might know the Spirit of Holy Scripture thoroughly, drinking it in, till we are saturated with it! This is the blessing which we resolve to obtain.

*By God's grace we purpose to believe the Word of God more intensely.* There is believing, and believing. You believe in all your brethren here assembled, but in some of them you have a conscious practical confidence, since in your hour of trouble they have come to your rescue and proved themselves brothers born for adversity. You confide in these, with absolute certitude, because you have personally tried them. Your faith was faith before; but now it is a higher, firmer, and more assured confidence. Believe in the inspired volume up to the hilt. Believe it right through; believe it thoroughly; believe it with the whole strength of your being. Let the truths of Scripture become the chief factors in your life, the chief operative forces of your action. Let the great transactions of the gospel story be to you as really and practically facts, as any fact which meets you in the domestic circle, or in the outside world: let them be as vividly true to you as your own ever present body, with its aches and pains, its appetites and joys. If we can get out of the realm of fiction and fancy, into the world of fact, we shall have struck a vein of power which will yield us countless treasure of strength. Thus, to become 'mighty in the Scriptures' will be to become 'mighty through God.'

*We should resolve also that we will quote more of Holy Scripture.* Sermons should be full of Bible; sweetened, strengthened, sanctified with Bible essence. The kind of sermons that people need to hear are outgrowths of Scripture. If they do not love to hear them, there is all the more reason why they should be preached to them. The gospel has the singular faculty of creating a taste for itself. Bible hearers, when they hear indeed, come to be Bible lovers. The mere stringing of texts together is a poor way of making sermons; though some have tried it, and I doubt not God has blessed them, since they did their best. It is far better to string texts together, than to pour out one's own poor thoughts in a washy flood. There will at least be something to be thought of and remembered if the Holy Word be quoted; and in the other case there may be nothing whatever. Texts of Scripture need not, however, be strung together, they may be fitly brought in to give edge and point to a discourse. They will be the force of the sermon. Our own words are mere paper pellets compared with the rifle shot of the Word. The Scripture is the conclusion of the whole matter. There is no arguing after we find that 'It is written.' To a large extent in the hearts and consciences of our hearers debate is over when the Lord has spoken. 'Thus saith the Lord' is the end of discussion to Christian minds; and even the ungodly cannot resist Scripture without resisting the Spirit who wrote it. That we may speak convincingly we will speak Scripturally.

*We are further resolved that we will preach nothing but the Word of God.* The alienation of the masses from hearing the gospel is largely to be accounted for by the sad fact that it is not always the gospel that they hear if they go to places of worship; and all else falls short of what their souls need. Have you never heard of a king who made a series of great feasts, and bade many, week after week? He had a number of servants who were appointed to wait at his table; and these went forth on the appointed days, and spake with the people. But, somehow, after a while the bulk of the people did not come to the feasts. They came in decreasing number; but the great mass of citizens turned their backs on the banquets. The king made enquiry, and he found that the food provided did not seem to satisfy the men who came to look upon the banquets; and so they came no more. He determined himself to examine the tables and the meats placed thereon. He saw much finery and many pieces of display which never came out of his storehouses. He looked at the food and he said, 'But how is this? These dishes, how came they here? These are not of my providing. My oxen and fatlings were killed, yet we have not here the flesh of fed beasts, but hard meat from cattle lean and starved. Bones are here, but where is the fat and the marrow? The bread also is coarse; whereas mine was made of the finest wheat. The wine is mixed with water, and the water is not from a pure well.' One of those who stood by answered and said, 'O king, we thought that the people would be surfeited with marrow and fatness, and so we gave them bone and gristle to try their teeth upon. We thought also that they would be weary of the best white bread, and so we baked a little at our own homes, in which the bran and husks were allowed to remain. It is the opinion of the learned that our provision is more suitable for these times than that which your majesty prescribed so long ago. As for the wines on the lees, the taste of men runs not that way in this age; and so transparent a liquid as pure water is too light a draught for men who are wont to drink of the river of Egypt, which has a taste in it of mud from the Mountains of the Moon.' Then the king knew why the people came not to the feast. Does the reason why going to the house of God has become so distasteful to a great many of the population, lie in this direction? I believe it does. Have our Lord's servants been chopping up their own odds and ends and tainted bits, to make therewith a potted meat for the millions; and do the millions therefore turn away? Listen to the rest of my parable. 'Clear the tables!' cried the king in indignation: 'Cast that rubbish to the dogs. Bring in the barons of beef: set forth my royal provender. Remove those gewgaws from the hall, and that adulterated bread from the table, and cast out the water of the muddy river.' They did so; and if my parable is right, very soon there was a rumour throughout the streets that truly royal dainties were to be had, and the people thronged the palace, and the king's name became exceeding great throughout the land. Let us try the plan. Maybe, we shall soon rejoice to see our Master's banquet furnished with guests.

We are resolved, then, to use more fully than ever what God has provided for us in this Book, for *we are sure of its inspiration.* Let me say that over again. **We are sure of its inspiration.** You will notice that attacks are frequently made as against *verbal* inspiration. The form chosen is a mere pretext. Verbal inspiration is the verbal form of the assault, but the attack is really aimed at inspiration itself. You will not read far in the essay before you will find that the gentleman who started with contesting a theory of inspiration which none of us ever held, winds up by showing his hand, and that hand wages war with inspiration itself. There is the true point. We care little for any theory of inspiration: in fact, we have none. To us the plenary verbal inspiration of Holy Scripture is fact, and not hypothesis. It is a pity to theorize upon a subject which is deeply mysterious, and makes a demand upon faith rather than fancy. Believe in the inspiration of Scripture, and believe it in the most intense sense. You will not believe in a truer and fuller inspiration than really exists. No one is likely to err in that direction, even if error be possible. If you adopt theories which pare off a portion here, and deny authority to a passage there, you will at last have no inspiration left, worthy of the name.

*If this book be not infallible, where shall we find infallibility?* We have given up the Pope, for he has blundered often and terribly; but we shall not set up instead of him a horde of little popelings fresh from college. Are these correctors of Scripture infallible? Is it certain that our Bibles are not right, but that the critics must be so? The old silver is to be depreciated; but the German silver, which is put in its place, is to be taken at the value of gold. Striplings fresh from reading the last new novel correct the notions of their fathers, who were men of weight and character. Doctrines which produced the godliest generation that ever lived on the face of the earth are scouted as sheer folly. Nothing is so obnoxious to these creatures as that which has the smell of Puritanism upon it. Every little man's nose goes up celestially at the very sound of the word 'Puritan'; though if the Puritans were here again, they would not dare to treat them thus cavalierly; for if Puritans did fight, they were soon known as Ironsides, and their leader could hardly be called a fool, even by those who stigmatized him as a 'tyrant'. Cromwell, and they that were with him, were not all weak-minded persons—surely? Strange that these are lauded to the skies by the very men who deride their true successors, believers in the same faith. But where shall infallibility be found? 'The depth saith, it is not in me'; yet those who have no depth at all would have us imagine that it is in them; or else by perpetual change they hope to hit upon it. Are we now to believe that infallibility is with learned men? Now, Farmer Smith, when you have read your Bible, and have enjoyed its precious promises, you will have, to-morrow morning, to go down the street to ask the scholarly man at the parsonage whether this portion of the Scripture belongs to the inspired part of the Word, or whether it is of dubious authority. It will be well for you to know whether it was written by *the* Isaiah, or whether it was by the second of the 'two Obadiahs.' All possibility of certainty is transferred from the spiritual man to a class of persons whose scholarship is pretentious, but who do not even pretend to spirituality. We shall gradually be so bedoubted and becriticized, that only a few of the most profound will know what is Bible, and what is not, and they will dictate to all the rest of us. I have no more faith in their mercy than in their accuracy: they will rob us of all that we hold most dear, and glory in the cruel deed. This same reign of terror we shall not endure, for we still believe that God revealeth Himself rather to babes than to the wise and prudent, and we are fully assured that our own old English version of the Scriptures is sufficient for plain men for all purposes of life, salvation, and godliness. We do not despise learning, but we will never say of culture or criticism. 'These be thy gods, O Israel!'

Do you see why men would lower the degree of inspiration in Holy Writ, and would fain reduce it to an infinitesimal quantity? It is because the truth of God is to be supplanted. If you ever go into a shop in the evening to buy certain goods which depend so much upon colour and texture as to be best judged of by daylight; if, after you have got into the shop, the tradesman proceeds to lower the gas, or to remove the lamp, and then commences to show you his goods, your suspicion is aroused, and you conclude that he will try to palm off an inferior article. I more than suspect this to be the little game of the inspiration-depreciators. Whenever a man begins to lower your view of inspiration, it is because he has a trick to play, which is not easily performed in the light. He would hold a *séance* of evil spirits, and therefore he cries, 'Let the lights be lowered.' We, brethren, are willing to ascribe to the Word of God all the inspiration that can possibly be ascribed to it; and we say boldly that if our preaching is not according to this Word, it is because there is no light in it. We are willing to be tried and tested by it in every way, and we count those to be the noblest of our hearers who search the Scriptures daily to see whether these things be so; but to those who belittle inspiration we will give place by subjection, no, not for an hour.

Do I hear someone say, 'But still you must submit to the conclusions of science'? No one is more ready than we are to accept the evident *facts* of science. But what do you mean by science? Is the thing called 'science'

infallible? Is it not science 'falsely so-called'?
The history of that human ignorance which
calls itself 'philosophy' is absolutely identical
with the history of fools, except where it
diverges into madness. If another Erasmus
were to arise and write the history of folly,
he would have to give several chapters
to philosophy and science, and those
chapters would be more telling than any
others. I should not myself dare to say that
philosophers and scientists are generally
fools; but I would give them liberty to speak
of one another, and at the close I would say,
'Gentlemen, you are less complimentary to
each other than I should have been.' I would
let the wise of each generation speak of the
generation that went before it, or nowadays
each half of a generation might deal with the
previous half generation; for there is little of
theory in science to-day which will survive
twenty years, and only a little more which
will see the first day of the twentieth century.
We travel now at so rapid a rate that we rush
by sets of scientific hypotheses as quickly as
we pass telegraph posts when riding in an
express train. All that we are certain of to-
day is this, that what the learned were sure

of a few years ago is now thrown into the limbo of discarded errors. I believe in science, but not in what is called 'science.' No proven fact in nature is opposed to revelation. The pretty speculations of the pretentious we cannot reconcile with the Bible, and would not if we could. I feel like the man who said, 'I can understand in some degree how these great men have found out the weight of the stars, and their distances from one another, and even how, by the spectroscope, they have discovered the materials of which they are composed; but', said he, 'I cannot guess how they found out their names.' Just so. The fanciful part of science, so dear to many, is what we do not accept. That is the important part of science to many—that part which is a mere guess, for which the guessers fight tooth and nail. The mythology of science is as false as the mythology of the heathen; but this is thing which is made a god of. I say again, as far as its facts are concerned, science is never in conflict with the truths of Holy Scripture, but the hurried deductions drawn from those facts, and the inventions classed as facts, are opposed to Scripture, and necessarily so, because falsehood agrees not with truth.

Two sorts of people have wrought great mischief, and yet they are neither of them worth being considered as judges in the matter: they are both of them disqualified. It is essential than an umpire should know both sides of a question, and neither of these is thus instructed. The first is the irreligious scientist. What does he know about religion? What can he know? He is out of court when the question is—Does science agree with religion? Obviously he who would answer this query must know both of the two things in the question. The second is a better man, but capable of still more mischief. I mean the unscientific Christian, who will trouble his head about reconciling the Bible with science. He had better leave it alone, and not begin his tinkering trade. The mistake made by such men has been that in trying to solve a difficulty, they have either twisted the Bible, or contorted science. The solution has soon been seen to be erroneous, and then we hear the cry that Scripture has been defeated. Not at all; not at all. It is only a vain gloss upon it which has been removed. Here is a good brother who writes a tremendous book, to prove that the six days of creation represent six great geological periods; and he shows how the geological strata, and the organisms thereof, follow very much in the order of the Genesis story of creation. It may be so, or it may be not so; but if anybody should before long show that the strata do not lie in any such order, what would be my reply? I should say that the Bible never taught that they did. The Bible said, 'In the beginning God created the heaven and the earth.' That leaves any length of time for your fire-ages and your ice-periods, and all that, before the establishment of the present age of man.[8] Then we reach the six days in which the Lord made the heavens and the earth, and rested on the seventh day. There is nothing said about long ages of time, but, on the contrary, 'the evening and the morning were the first day', and 'the evening and the morning were the second day'; and so on. I do not here lay down any theory, but simply say that if our friend's great book is all fudge, the Bible is not responsible for it. It is true that his theory has an appearance of support from the parallelism which he makes out between the organic life of the ages and that of the seven

---

8.  This is the Gap Theory which was popular in the late nineteenth century, but is less so now.

days; but this may be accounted for from the fact that God usually follows a certain order whether he works in long periods or short ones. I do not know, and I do not care, much about the question; but I want to say that, if you smash up an explanation you must not imagine that you have damaged the Scriptural truth which seemed to require the explanation: you have only burned the wooden palisades with which well-meaning men thought to protect an impregnable fort which needed no such defence. For the most part, we had better leave a difficulty where it is, rather than make another difficulty by our theory. Why make a second hole in the kettle, to mend the first? Especially when the first hole is not there at all, and needs no mending. Believe everything in science which is proved: it will not come to much. You need not fear that your faith will be over-burdened. And then believe everything which is clearly in the Word of God, whether it is proved by outside evidence or not. No proof is needed when God speaks. If He hath said it, this is evidence enough.

But we are told that we ought to give up a part of our old-fashioned theology to save the rest. We are in a carriage travelling over the steppes of Russia. The horses are being driven furiously, but the wolves are close upon us! Can you not see their eyes of fire? The danger is pressing. What must we do? It is proposed that we throw out a child or two. By the time they have eaten the baby, we shall have made a little headway; but should they again overtake us, what then? Why, brave man, *throw out your wife!* 'All that a man hath will he give for his life'; give up nearly every truth in hope of saving one. Throw out inspiration, and let the critics devour it. Throw out election, and all the old Calvinism; here will be a dainty feast for the wolves, and the gentlemen who give us the sage advice will be glad to see the doctrines of grace torn limb from limb. Throw out natural depravity, eternal punishment, and the efficacy of prayer. We have lightened the carriage wonderfully. Now for another drop. *Sacrifice the great sacrifice!* Have done with the atonement!

Brethren, this advice is villainous, and murderous; we will escape these wolves with everything, or we will be lost with everything. It shall be 'the truth, the whole truth, and nothing but the truth', or none at all. We will never attempt to save half the truth by casting any part of it away. The sage advice which has been given us involves treason to God, and disappointment to ourselves. We will stand by all or none. We are told that if we give up something the adversaries will also give up something; but we care not what they will do, for we are not in the least afraid of them. They are not the Imperial conquerors they think themselves. We ask no quarter from their insignificance. We are of the mind of the warrior who was offered presents to buy him off, and he was told that if he accepted so much gold or territory he could return home in triumph, and glory in his easy gain. But he said, 'The Greeks set no store by concessions. They find their glory not in presents, but in spoils.' We shall with the sword of the Spirit maintain the whole truth as ours, and shall not accept a part of it as a grant from the enemies of God. The truth of God we will maintain *as the truth of God,* and we shall not retain it because the philosophic mind consents to our doing so. If scientists agree to our believing a part of the Bible, we thank them for nothing: we believe it whether or no. Their assent is of no more consequence to our faith than the consent of a Frenchman to the Englishman's holding London, or the consent of the mole to the eagle's sight. God being with us, we shall not cease from this glorying, but will hold the whole of revealed truth, even to the end.

But now, brethren, while keeping to this first part of my theme, perhaps at too great a length, I say to you that, *believing this, we accept the obligation to preach everything which we see to be in the Word of God, as far as we see it.* We would not wilfully leave out any portion of the whole revelation of God, but we long to be able to say at the last, 'We have not shunned to declare unto you the whole counsel of God.' What mischief may come of leaving out any portion of the truth, or putting in an alien element! All good men will not agree with me when I say that the addition of infant baptism to the Word of God—for it certainly is not there—is fraught with mischief. Baptismal regeneration rides in upon the shoulders of Pedobaptism. But I speak now of what I know. I have received letters from missionaries, not Baptists, but Wesleyans and Congregationalists, who have said to me, 'Since we have been here' (I will not mention the localities lest I get the good men into trouble) 'we find a class of persons who are the children of former converts, and who have been baptized, and are therefore called Christians; but they are not one whit better than the heathen around them. They seem to think that they are Christians because of their baptism, and at the same time, being thought Christians by the heathen, their evil lives are perpetual scandal and a dreadful stumbling-block.' In many cases this must be so. I only use the fact as an illustration. But suppose it to be either some other error invented, or some great truth neglected, evil will come of it. In the case of the terrible truths known by us as 'the terrors of the Lord'; their omission is producing the saddest results. A good man, whom we do not accept as teaching exactly the truth upon this solemn matter, has, nevertheless, most faithfully written again and again to the papers to say that the great weakness of the modern pulpit is that it ignores the justice of God and the punishment of sin. His witness is true, and the evil which he indicates is incalculably great. You cannot leave out that part of the truth which is so dark and so solemn without weakening the force of all the others' truths you preach. You rob of their brightness, and their urgent importance, the truths which concern salvation from the wrath to come. Brethren, leave out nothing. Be bold enough to preach unpalatable and unpopular truth. The evil which we may do by adding to, or taking from the Word of the Lord, may not happen in our own days; but if it should come to ripeness in another generation we shall be equally guilty. I have no doubt that the omission of certain truths by the earlier churches led afterwards to serious error; while certain additions in the form of rites and ceremonies, which appeared innocent enough in themselves, led up to Ritualism, and afterwards to the great apostasy of Romanism! Be very careful. Do not go an inch beyond the line of Scripture, and do not stay an inch on this side of it. Keep to the straight line of the Word of God, as far as the Holy Spirit has taught you, and hold back nothing which He has revealed. Be not so bold as to abolish the two ordinances which the Lord Jesus has ordained, though some have ventured upon that gross presumption; neither exaggerate those ordinances into inevitable channels of grace, as others have superstitiously done. Keep you to the revelation of the Spirit. Remember, you will have to give an account, and that account will not be with joy if you have played false with God's truth. Remember the story of Gylippus, to whom Lysander entrusted bags of gold to take to the city authorities. Those bags were tied at the mouth, and then sealed; and Gylippus thought that if he cut the bags at the bottom he might extract a part of the coin, and then he could carefully sew the bottom up again, and so the seals would not be broken, and no one would suspect that gold had been taken. When the bags were opened, to his horror and surprise, there was a note in each bag stating how much it should contain, and so he was detected. The Word of God has self-verifying clauses in it, so that you cannot run away with a part of it, without the remainder of it accusing and convicting you. How will you answer for it 'in that day', if you have added to, or taken from the Word of the Lord? I am not here to decide what you ought to consider to be the truth of God; but, whatever you judge it to be, preach it all, and preach it definitely and plainly. If I differ from you, or you from me, we shall not differ very much, if we are equally honest, straightforward, and God-fearing. The way to peace is not concealment of convictions, but the honest expression of them in the power of the Holy Ghost.

One more word. *We accept the obligation to preach all that is in God's Word, definitely and distinctly.* Do not many preach indefinitely, handling the Word of God deceitfully? You might attend upon their ministry for years and not know what they believe. I heard concerning a certain cautious minister, that he was asked by a hearer, 'What is your view of the atonement?' He answered, 'My dear sir, that is just what I have never told to anybody, and you are not going to get it out of me.' This is a strange moral condition for the mind of a preacher of the gospel. I fear that he is not alone in this reticence. They say 'they consume their own smoke'; that is to say, they keep their doubts for home consumption. Many dare not say in the pulpit what they say *sub rosâ,*[9] at a private meeting of ministers. Is this honest? I am afraid that it is with some as it was with the schoolmaster in one of the

---

9.　which means 'privately'

towns of a Southern state in America. A grand old black preacher, one Jasper, had taught his people that the world is as flat as a pancake, and that the sun goes round it every day. This part of his teaching we do not receive; but certain persons had done so, and one of them going to a schoolmaster with his boy, asked, 'Do you teach the children that the world is round or flat?' The schoolmaster cautiously answered, 'Yes.' The enquirer was puzzled, but asked for a clearer answer. 'Do you teach your children that the world is round, or that the world is flat?' Then one American dominie answered, '*That* depends upon the opinions of the parents.' I suspect that even in Great Britain, in some few cases, a good deal depends upon the leaning of the leading deacon, or the principal subscriber, or the gilded youth in the congregation. If it be so, the crime is loathsome.

But whether for this or for any other cause we teach with double tongue, the result will be highly injurious. I venture here to quote a story which I heard from a beloved brother. A cadger called upon a minister to extract money from him. The good man did not like the beggar's appearance much, and he said to him, 'I do not care for your case, and I see no special reason why you should come to me.' The beggar replied, 'I am sure you would help me if you knew what great benefit I have received from your blessed ministry.' 'What is that?' said the pastor. The beggar then replied, 'Why, sir, when I first came to hear you I cared neither for God nor devil, but now, under your blessed ministry, *I have come to love them both.*' What marvel if, under some men's shifty talk, people grow into love of both truth and falsehood! People will say, 'We like this form of doctrine, and we like the other also.' The fact is, they would like anything if only a clever deceiver would put it plausibly before them. They admire Moses and Aaron, but they would not say a word against Jannes and Jambres. We shall not join in the confederacy which seems to aim at such a comprehension. We must preach the gospel so distinctly that our people know what we are preaching. 'If the trumpet give an uncertain sound, who shall prepare himself for the battle?'[10] Don't puzzle your people with doubtful speeches. 'Well', said one, 'I had a new idea the other day. I did

---

10. 1 Corinthians 14:8.

not enlarge upon it; but I just threw it out.' That is a very good thing to do with most of your new ideas. Throw them out, by all means; but mind where you are when you do it; for if you throw them out from the pulpit they may strike somebody, and inflict a wound upon faith. Throw out your fancies, but first go alone in a boat a mile out to sea. When you have once thrown out your unconsidered trifles, leave them to the fishes.

We have nowadays around us a class of men who preach Christ, and even preach the gospel; but then they preach a great deal else which is not true, and thus they destroy the good of all that they deliver, and lure men to error. They would be styled 'evangelical' and yet be of the school which is really anti-evangelical. Look well to these gentlemen. I have heard that a fox, when close hunted by the dogs, will pretend to be one of them, and run with the pack. That is what certain are aiming at just now: *the foxes would seem to be dogs.* But in the case of the fox, his strong scent betrays him, and the dogs soon find him out; and even so, the scent of false doctrine is not easily concealed, and the game does not answer for long. There are extant ministers of whom we scarce can tell whether they are dogs or foxes; but all men shall know our quality as long as we live, and they shall be in no doubt as to what we believe and teach. We shall not hesitate to speak in the strongest Saxon words we can find, and in the plainest sentences we can put together, that which we hold as fundamental truth.

Thus I have been all this while upon my first head, and the other two must, therefore, occupy less time, though I judge them to be of the first importance.

# 2

# Our Army

Now we must review **our army**.

What can individual men do in a great crusade? We are associated with all the people of the Lord. We need for comrades the members of our churches; these must go out and win souls for Christ. We need the co-operation of the entire brotherhood and sisterhood. What is to be accomplished unless the saved ones go forth, all of them, for the salvation of others? But the question now is mooted, *Is there to be a church at all?* Is there to be a distinct army of saints, or are we to include atheists? You have heard of 'the church of the future' which we are to have *instead* of the church of Jesus Christ. As its extreme lines will take in atheists, we may hope, in our charity, that it will include evil spirits also. What a wonderful church it will be, certainly, when we see it! It will be anything else you like, but not a church. When the soldiers of Christ shall have included in their ranks all the banditti of the adversary, will there be any army for Christ at all? Is it not distinctly a capitulation at the very beginning of the war? So I take it to be.

We must not only believe in the church of God, but recognize it very distinctly. Some denominations recognize anything and every-thing more than the church. Such a thing as a meeting of the church is unknown. In some 'the church' signifies the ministers or clergy; but in truth it should signify the whole body of the faithful, and there should be an opportunity for these to meet together to act as a church. It is, I judge, for the church of God to carry on the work of God in the land. The final power and direction is with our Lord Jesus, and under Him it should lie, not with some few who are chosen by delegation or by patronage, but with the whole body of believers. We must more and more acknowledge the church which God has committed to our charge; and in so doing, we shall evoke a strength which else lies dormant. If the church is recognized by Christ Jesus, it is worthy to be recognized by us; for we are the servants of the church.

Yes, we believe that there ought to be a church. But churches are very disappointing things. Every pastor of a large church will own this in his own soul. I do not know that the churches of to-day are any worse than they used to be in Paul's time, or any better. The churches at Corinth and Laodicea and other cities exhibited grave faults; and if there are faults in ours, let us not be amazed; but yet let us grieve over such things, and labour after a higher standard. Albeit that the members of our church are not all they ought to be, neither are we ourselves. Yet, if I went anywhere for choice company, I should certainly resort to the members of my church.

These are the company I keep:
These are the choicest friends I know.

O Jerusalem, with all thy faults, I love thee still! The people of God are still the aristocracy of the race: God bless them! Yes, we mean to have a church.

Now, *is that church to be real or statistical?* That depends very much upon you, dear brethren. I would urge upon you the resolve to have no church unless it be a real one. The fact is, that too frequently religious statistics are shockingly false. Cooking of such accounts is not an unknown art in certain quarters, as we know. I heard of one case the other day where an increase of four was reported; but had the roll been amended in the least, there must have been a decrease of twenty-five. Is it not falsehood when numbers are manipulated? There is a way of making figures figure as they should not figure. Never do this. Let us not keep names on our books when they are only names. Certain of the good old people like to keep them there, and cannot bear to have them removed; but when you do not know where individuals are, nor what they are, how can you count them? They are gone to America, or Australia, or to heaven, but as far as your roll is concerned they are with you still. Is this a right thing? It may not be possible to be absolutely accurate, but let us aim at it. We ought to look upon this in a very serious light, and purge ourselves of the vice of false reporting; for God Himself will not bless mere names. It is not His way to work with those who play a false part. If there is not a real person for each name, amend your list. Keep your church real and effective, or make no report. A merely nominal church is a lie. Let it be what it professes to be. We may not glory in statistics; but we ought to know the facts.

*But is this church to increase, or is it to die out?* It will do either the one or the other. We shall see our friends going to heaven, and, if there are no young men and young women converted and brought in and added to us, the church on earth will have emigrated to the church triumphant above; and what is to be done for the cause and the kingdom of the Master here below? We should be crying, praying, and pleading that the church may continually grow. We must preach, visit, pray, and labour for this end. May the Lord add unto us daily such as are saved! If there be no harvest, can the seed be the true seed? Are we preaching apostolic doctrine if we never see apostolic results? Oh, my brethren, our hearts should be ready to break if there be no increase in the flocks we tend. O Lord, we beseech Thee, send now prosperity!

If a church is to be what it ought to be for the purposes of God, *we must train it in the holy art of prayer.* Churches without prayer-meetings are grievously common. Even if there were only one such, it would be one to weep over. In many churches the prayer-meeting is only the skeleton of a gathering: the form is kept up, but the people do not come. There is no interest, no power, in connection with the meeting. Oh, my brothers, let it not be so with you! Do train the people to continually meet together for prayer. Rouse them to incessant supplication. There is a holy art in it. Study to show yourselves approved by the prayerfulness of your people. If you pray yourself, you will want them to pray with you; and when they begin to pray with you, and for you, and for the work of the Lord, they will want more prayer themselves, and the appetite will grow. Believe me, if a church does not pray, it is dead. Instead of putting united prayer last, put it first. Everything will hinge upon the power of prayer in the church.

*We ought to have our churches all busy for God.* What is the use of a church that simply assembles to hear sermons, even as a family gathers to eat its meals? What, I say, is the profit, if it does no work? Are not many professors sadly indolent in the Lord's work, though diligent enough in their own? Because of

Christian idleness we hear of the necessity for amusements, and all sorts of nonsense. If they were at work for the Lord Jesus we should not hear of this. A good woman said to a housewife, 'Mrs. So-and-so, how do you manage to amuse yourself?' 'Why', she replied, 'my dear, you see there are so many children that there is much work to be done in my house.' 'Yes', said the other, 'I see it. I see that there is much work to be done in your house; but as it never is done, I was wondering how you amused yourself.' Much needs to be done by a Christian church within its own bounds, and for the neighbourhood, and for the poor and the fallen, and for the heathen world, and so forth; and if it is well attended to, minds, and hearts, and hands, and tongues will be occupied, and diversions will not be asked for. Let idleness come in, and that spirit which rules lazy people, and there will arise a desire to be amused. What amusements they are, too! If religion is not a farce with some congregations, at any rate they turn out better to see a farce than to unite in prayer. I cannot understand it. The man who is all aglow with love to Jesus finds little need for amusement. He has no time for trifling. He is in dead earnest to save souls, and establish the truth, and enlarge the kingdom of his Lord. There has always been some pressing claim for the cause of God upon me; and, that settled, there has been another, and another, and another, and the scramble has been to find opportunity to do the work that must be done, and hence I have not had the time for gadding abroad after frivolities. Oh, to get a working church! The German churches, when our dear friend, Mr. Oncken, was alive, always carried out the rule of asking every member, 'What are you going to do for Christ?' and they put the answer down in a book. The one thing that was required of every member was that he should continue doing something for the Saviour. If he ceased to do anything it was a matter for church discipline, for he was an idle professor, and could not be allowed to remain in the church like a drone in a hive of working bees. He must do or go. Oh, for a vineyard without a barren fig-tree to cumber the ground! At present the most of our sacred warfare is carried on by a small body of intensely living, earnest people, and the rest are either in hospital, or are mere camp followers. We are thankful for that consecrated few; but we pine to see the altar fire consuming all that is professedly laid upon the altar.

Brethren, *we want churches also that produce saints;* men of mighty faith and prevalent prayer; men of holy living, and of consecrated giving; men filled with the Holy Spirit. We must have these saints as rich clusters, or surely we are not branches of the true vine. I would desire to see in every church a Mary sitting at Jesus' feet, a Martha serving Jesus, a Peter and a John; but the best name for a church is 'All Saints.' All believers should be saints, and all may be saints. We have no connection with 'the latter-day saints', but we love everyday saints. Oh, for more of them! If God shall so help us that the whole company of the faithful shall, each one of them individually, come to the fulness of the stature of a man in Christ Jesus, then we shall see greater things than these. Glorious times will come when believers have glorious characters.

*We want also churches that know the truth, and are well taught in the things of God.* What do some Christian people know? They come and hear, and, in the plenitude of your wisdom, you instruct them; but how little they receive to lay by in store for edification! Brethren, the fault lies partly with us, and partly with themselves. If we taught better they would learn better. See how little many professors know; not enough to give them discernment between living truth and deadly error. Old-fashioned believers could give you chapter and verse for what they believed; but how few of such remain! Our venerable grandsires were at home when conversing upon 'the covenants.' I love men who love the covenant of grace, and base their divinity upon it: the doctrine of the covenants is the key of theology. They that feared the Lord spake often one to another. They used to speak of everlasting life, and all that comes of it. They had a good argument for this belief, and an excellent reason for that other doctrine; and to try to shake them was by no means a hopeful task: you might as well have hoped to shake the pillars of the universe; for they were steadfast, and could not be carried about with every wind of doctrine. They knew what they knew, and they held fast that which they had learned. What is to become of our country, with the present deluge of Romanism pouring upon us through the ritualistic party, unless our churches abound in firm believers who can discern between the regeneration of the Holy Spirit and its ceremonial substitute? What is to become of our churches in this day of scepticism, when every fixed truth is pointed at with the finger of doubt, unless our people have the truths of the gospel written in their hearts? Oh, for a church of out-and-out believers, impervious to the soul-destroying doubt which pours upon us in showers!

Yet all this would not reach our ideal. *We want a church of a missionary character,* which will go forth to gather out a people unto God from all parts of the world. A church is a soul-saving company, or it is nothing. If the salt exercises no preserving influence on that which surrounds it, what is the use of it? Yet some shrink from effort in their immediate neighbourhood because of the poverty and vice of the people. I remember a minister who is now deceased, a very good man he was, too, in many respects; but he utterly amazed me by a reply which he made to a question of mine. I remarked that he had an awful neighbourhood round his chapel, and, I said, 'Are you able to do much for them?' He answered, 'No, I feel almost glad that we keep clear of them; for, you see, if any of them were converted, it would be a fearful burden upon us.' I knew him to be the soul of caution and prudence, but this took me aback, and I sought an explanation. 'Well,' he said, 'we should have to keep them: they are mostly thieves and harlots, and if converted they would have no means of livelihood, and we are a poor people, and could not support them'! He was a devout man, and one with whom it was to one's profit to converse; and yet that was how he had gradually come to look at the case. His people with difficulty sustained the expenses of worship, and thus chill penury repressed a gracious zeal, and froze the genial current of his soul. There was a great deal of common sense in what he said, but yet it was an awful thing to be able to say it. We want a people who will not for ever sing,—

> We are a garden walled around,
> Chosen and made peculiar ground;
> A little spot enclosed by grace,
> Out of the world's wild wilderness.

It is good verse for occasional singing, but not when it comes to mean, 'We are very few, and we wish to be.' No, no, brethren! we are a little detachment of the King's soldiers detained in a foreign country upon garrison duty; yet we mean not only to hold the fort, but to add territory to our Lord's dominion. We are not to be driven out; but, on the contrary, we are going to drive out the Canaanites; for this land belongs to us, it is given to us of the Lord, and we will subdue it. May we be fired with the spirit of discoverers and conquerors, and never rest while there yet remains a class to be rescued, a region to be evangelized!

We are rowing like lifeboat men upon a stormy sea, and we are hurrying to yonder wreck, where men are perishing. If we may not draw that old wreck to shore, we will at least, by the power of God, rescue the perishing, save life, and bear the redeemed to the shores of salvation. Our mission, like our Lord's, is to gather out the chosen of God from among men, that they may live to the glory of God. Every saved man should be, under God, a saviour; and the church is not in a right state until she has reached that conception of herself. The elect church is saved that she may save, cleansed that she may cleanse, blessed that she may bless. All the world is the field, and all the members of the church should work therein for the great Husbandman. Waste lands are to be reclaimed, and forests broken up by the plough, till the solitary place begins to blossom as the rose. We must not be content with holding our own: we must invade the territories of the prince of darkness.

My brethren, what is our relation to this church? What is our position in it? *We are servants.* May we always know our place, and keep it! The highest place in the church will always come to the man who willingly chooses the lowest; while he that aspires to be great among his brethren will sink to be least of all. Certain men might have been something if they had not thought themselves so. A consciously great man is an evidently little one. A lord over God's heritage is a base usurper. He that in his heart and soul is always ready to serve the very least of the family; who expects to be put upon; and willingly sacrifices reputation and friendship for Christ's sake, he shall fulfil a heaven-sent ministry. We are not sent to be ministered unto, but to minister. Let us sing unto our Well-Beloved:

> There's not a lamb in all thy flock,
> I would disdain to feed;
> There's not a foe before whose face
> I'd fear thy cause to plead.

*We must also be examples to the flock.* He that cannot be safely imitated ought not to be tolerated in a pulpit. Did I hear of a minister who was always disputing for pre-eminence? Or of another who was mean and covetous? Or of a third whose conversation was not always chaste? Or of a fourth who did not rise, as a rule, till eleven o'clock in the morning? I would hope that this last rumour was altogether false. An idle minister—what will become of him? A pastor who neglects his office? Does he expect to go to heaven? I was about to say, 'If he does go there at all, may it be soon.' A lazy minister is a creature despised of men, and abhorred of God. 'You give your minister only £50 a year!' I said, to a farmer. 'Why, the poor man cannot live on it.' The answer was, 'Look here, sir! I tell you what: we give him a good deal more than he earns.' It is a sad pity when that can be said; it is an injury to all those who follow our sacred calling. We are to be examples to our flock in all things. In all diligence, in all gentleness, in all humility, and in all holiness we are to excel. When Caesar went on his wars, one thing always helped his soldiers to bear hardships: they knew that Caesar fared as they fared. He marched if they marched, he thirsted if they thirsted, and he was always in the heart of the battle if they were fighting. We must do more than others if we are officers in Christ's army. We must not cry, 'Go on', but, 'Come on.' Our people may justly expect of us, at the very least, that we should be among the most self-denying, the most laborious, and the most earnest in the church, *and somewhat more*. We cannot expect to see holy churches if we who are bound to be their examples are unsanctified. If there be, in any of our brethren, consecration and sanctification, evident to all men, God has blessed them, and God will bless them more and more. If these be lacking in us, we need not search far to find the cause of our non-success.

I have many things to say to you, but you cannot bear them now, because the time is long and you are weary. I desire, however, if you can gather up your patience and your strength, to dwell for a little upon the most important part of my triple theme. Here suffer me to pray for His help, whose name and person I would magnify. Come, Holy Spirit, heavenly Dove, and rest upon us now!

# 3

# Our Strength

**G**ranted that we preach the Word alone; granted that we are surrounded by a model church, which, alas, is not always the case; but, granted that it is so, **our strength** is the next consideration. This must come from the **Spirit of God**. We believe in the Holy Ghost, and in our absolute dependence upon Him. We believe; but do we believe *practically*? Brethren, as to ourselves and our own work, do we believe in the Holy Ghost? Do we believe because we habitually prove the truth of the doctrine?

*We must depend upon the Spirit in our preparations.* Is this the fact with us all? Are you in the habit of working your way into the meaning of texts by the guidance of the Holy Spirit? Every man that goes to the land of heavenly knowledge must work his passage thither; but he must work out his passage in the strength of the Holy Spirit, or he will arrive at some island in the sea of fancy, and never set his foot upon the sacred shores of the truth. You do not know the truth, my brother, because you have read 'Hodge's Outlines', or 'Fuller's Gospel worthy of all Acceptation'; or 'Owen on the Spirit', or any other classic of our faith. You do not know the truth, my brother, merely because you accept the Westminster Assembly's Confession, and have studied it perfectly. No, we know nothing till we are taught of the Holy Ghost, who speaks to the heart rather than to the ear. It is a wonderful fact that we do not even hear the voice of Jesus till the Spirit rests upon us. John says, 'I was in the Spirit on the Lord's day, and I heard a voice behind me.'[1] He heard not that voice till he was in the Spirit. How many heavenly words we miss because we abide not in the Spirit!

---

1.    Revelation 1:10.

We cannot succeed in supplication except the Holy Ghost helpeth our infirmities, for true prayer is 'praying in the Holy Ghost.' The Spirit makes an atmosphere around every living prayer, and within that circle prayer lives and prevails; outside of it prayer is a dead formality. As to ourselves, then, in our study, in prayer, in thought, in word, and in deed, we must depend upon the Holy Ghost.

*In the pulpit do we really and truly rest upon the aid of the Spirit?* I do not censure any brother for his mode of preaching, but I must confess that it seems very odd to me when a brother prays that the Holy Ghost may help him in preaching, and then I see him put his hand behind him and draw a manuscript out of his pocket, so fashioned that he can place it in the middle of his Bible, and read from it without being suspected of doing so. These precautions for ensuring secrecy look as though the man was a little ashamed of his paper; but I think he should be far more ashamed of his precautions. Does he expect the Spirit of God to bless him while he is practising a trick? And how can He help him when he reads out of a paper from which anyone else might read without the Spirit's aid? What has the Holy Ghost to do with the business? Truly, he may have had something to do with the manuscript in the composing of it, but in the pulpit His aid is superfluous. The truer thing would be to thank the Holy Spirit for assistance rendered, and ask that what He has enabled us to get into our pockets may now enter the people's hearts. Still, if the Holy Ghost should have anything to say to the people that is not in the paper, how can He say it by us? He seems to me to be very effectually blocked as to freshness of utterance by that method of ministry. Still, it is not for me to censure, although I may quietly plead for liberty in prophesying, and room for the Lord to give us in the same hour what we shall speak.

*Furthermore, we must depend upon the Spirit of God as to our results.* No man among us really thinks that he could regenerate a soul. We are not so foolish as to claim power to change a heart of stone. We may not dare to presume quite so far as this, and yet we may come to think that, by our experience, we can help people over spiritual difficulties. Can we? We may be hopeful that our enthusiasm will drive the living church before us, and drag the dead world after us. Will it be so? Perhaps we imagine that if we could only *get up* a revival, we should easily secure large additions to the church? Is it worth while to *get up* a revival? Are not all true revivals to be *got down?* We may persuade ourselves that drums and trumpets and shouting will do a great deal. But, my brethren, 'the Lord is not in the wind.' Results worth having come from that silent but omnipotent Worker whose name is the Spirit of God: in Him, and in Him only, must we trust for the conversion of a single Sunday-school child, and for every genuine revival. For the keeping of our people together, and for the building of them up into a holy temple, we must look to Him. The Spirit might say, even as our Lord did, 'Without me ye can do nothing.'

What is the Church of God without the Holy Ghost? Ask what would Hermon be without its dew, or Egypt without its Nile? Behold the land of Canaan when the curse of Elias fell upon it, and for three years it felt neither dew nor rain: such would Christendom become without the Spirit. What the valleys would be without their brooks, or the cities without their wells; what the corn-fields would be without the sun, or the vintage without the summer—that would our churches be without the Spirit. As well think of day without light, or life without breath, or heaven without God, as of Christian service without the Holy Spirit. Nothing can supply His place if He be absent: the pastures are a desert, the fruitful fields are a wilderness, Sharon languishes, and Carmel is burned with fire. Blessed Spirit of the Lord, forgive us that we have done Thee such despite, by our forgetfulness of Thee, by our proud self-sufficiency, by resisting Thine influences, and quenching Thy fire! Henceforth work in us according to Thine own excellence. Make our hearts tenderly impressible, and then turn us as wax to the seal, and stamp upon us the image of the Son of God. With some such prayer and confession of faith as this, let us pursue our subject in the power of the good Spirit of whom we speak.

What does the Holy Ghost do? Beloved, what is there of good work that He does not do? It is His to quicken, to convince, to illuminate, to cleanse, to guide, to preserve, to console, to confirm, to perfect, and to use. How much might be said under each one of these heads! It is He that worketh in us to will and to do. He that hath wrought all things is God. Glory be unto the Holy Ghost for all that He has accomplished in such poor, imperfect natures as ours! We can do nothing apart from the life-sap which flows to us from Jesus the Vine. That which is our own is fit only to cause us shame and confusion of face. We never go a step towards heaven without the Holy Ghost. We never lead another on the heavenward road without the Holy Ghost. We have no acceptable thought, or word, or deed, apart from the Holy Spirit. Even the uplifting of the eye and hope, or the ejaculatory prayer of the heart's desire, must be His work. All good things are of Him and through Him, from beginning to end. There is no fear of exaggerating here. Do we, however, translate this conviction into our actual procedure?

Instead of dilating upon what the Spirit of God does, let me refer to your experience, and ask you a question or two. Do you remember times when the Spirit of God has been graciously present in fulness of power with you and with your people?

What seasons those have been! That Sabbath was a high day. Those services were like the worship of Jacob when he said, 'Surely God was in this place!'[2] What mutual telegraphing goes on between the preacher in the Spirit and the people in the Spirit! Their eyes seem to talk to us as much as our tongues talk to them. They are then a very different people from what they are on common occasions: there is even a beauty upon their faces while we are glorifying the Lord Jesus, and they are enjoying and drinking in our testimony. Have you ever seen a gentleman of the modern school enjoying his own preaching? Our evangelical preachers are very happy in delivering what our liberal friends are pleased to call their 'platitudes'; but the moderns in their wisdom feel no such joy. Can you imagine a Downgrader in the glow which our Welsh friends call the *Hwyl?* How grimly they descant upon the *Post Exilic theory!* They remind me of Ruskin's expression— 'Turner had no joy of his mill.' I grant you, there is nothing to enjoy, and they are evidently glad to get through their task of piling up meatless bones. They stand at an

---

2.    Genesis 28:16.

empty manger, amusing themselves by biting
their crib. They get through their preaching,
and they are dull enough till Monday comes
with a football match, or an entertainment in
the school-room, or a political meeting. To
them preaching is 'work', though they don't
put much work into it. The old preachers,
and some of those who now live, but are said
to be 'obsolete', think the pulpit a throne,
or a triumphal chariot, and are near heaven
when helped to preach with power. Poor
fools that we are, preaching our 'antiquated'
gospel! We do enjoy the task. Our gloomy
doctrines make us very happy. Strange, is it
not? The gospel is evidently marrow and fatness to us, and our beliefs—albeit, of course,
they are very absurd and unphilosophical—
do content us, and make us very confident
and happy. I may say of some of my brethren, that their very eyes seem to sparkle, and
their souls to glow, while enlarging upon free
grace and dying love. It is so, brethren, that
when we have the presence of God, then we
and our hearers are carried away with heavenly delight. Nor is this all. When the Spirit
of God is present every saint loves his fellow
saint, and there is no strife among us unless it

be who shall be the most loving. Then prayer is wrestling and prevailing, and ministry is sowing good seed and reaping large sheaves. Then conversions are plentiful, restorations are abundant, and advances in grace are seen on every side. Hallelujah! With the Spirit of God all goes well.

But do you know the opposite condition? I hope you do not. It is death in life. I trust you have never, in your scientific experiments, been cruel enough to put a mouse under an air pump, and gradually to exhaust the receiver. I have read of the fatal experiment. Alas, poor mouse! As the air gets thinner and thinner, how great his sufferings, and when it is all gone, there he lies—dead. Have you never yourself been under an exhausted receiver, spiritually? You have only been there long enough to perceive that the sooner you escaped, the better for you. Said one to me the other day, 'Well, as to the sermon which I heard from the modern-thought divine, there was no great harm in it; for on this occasion he kept clear of false doctrine; but the whole affair was so intensely cold. I felt like a man who has fallen down a crevasse in a glacier: and I felt shut up as if I could not breathe the air of heaven.' You know that arctic cold; and it may occasionally be felt even where the doctrine is sound. When the Spirit of God is gone, even truth itself becomes an iceberg. How wretched is religion frozen and lifeless! The Holy Ghost has gone, and all energy and enthusiasm have gone with Him. The scene becomes like that described in the Ancient Mariner, when the ship was becalmed:—

> The very deep did rot,
> Alas, that ever this should be!
> Yea, slimy things did crawl with legs
> Upon the slimy sea.

Within the ship all was death. And we have seen it so within a church. I am tempted to apply Coleridge's lines to much that is to be seen in those churches which deserve the name of 'congregations of the dead.' He describes how the bodies of the dead were inspired and the ship moved on, each dead man fulfilling his office in a dead and formal fashion:

> The helmsman steered, the ship moved on;
> Yet never a breeze up blew;
> The mariners all 'gan work the ropes,

Where they were wont to do;
They raised their limbs like lifeless tools—
We were a ghastly crew.

All living fellowship was lacking, for the Ancient Mariner says:

The body of my brother's son
Stood by me, knee to knee:
The body and I pulled at one rope,
But he said nought to me.

It is much the same in those 'respectable' congregations where no man knows his fellow, and a dignified isolation supplants all saintly communion. To the preacher, if he be the only living man in the company, the church affords very dreary society. His sermons fall on ears that hear them not aright.

Twas night, calm night, the moon was high;
The dead men stood together.
All stood together on the deck
For a charnel-dungeon fitter:
All fixed on me their stony eyes,
That in the moon did glitter.

Yes, the preacher's moonlight, cold and cheerless, falls on faces which are like it. The discourse impresses their stolid intellects, and

fixes their stony eyes; but hearts! Well, hearts
are not in fashion in those regions. Hearts are
for the realm of life; but without the Holy
Spirit what do congregations know of true
life? If the Holy Ghost has gone, death reigns,
and the church is a sepulchre. Therefore we
must entreat Him to abide with us, and we
must never rest till He does so. O brothers, let
it not be that I talk to you about this, and that
then we permit the matter to drop; but let us
each one with heart and soul seek to have the
power of the Holy Spirit abiding upon him.

Have we received the Holy Ghost? Is He
with us now? If so it be, *how can we secure His
future presence?* How can we constrain Him
to abide with us?

I would say, first, *treat Him as He should
be treated.* Worship Him as the adorable Lord
God. Never call the Holy Spirit 'it'; nor
speak of Him as if He were a doctrine, or an
influence, or an orthodox myth. Reverence
Him, love Him, and trust Him with familiar
yet reverent confidence. He is God, let Him
be God to you.

*See to it that you act in conformity with His
working.* The mariner to the East cannot create
the winds at his pleasure, but he knows when

the trade winds blow, and he takes advantage of the season to speed his vessel. Put out to sea in holy enterprise when the heavenly wind is with you. Take the sacred tide at its flood. Increase your meetings when you feel that the Spirit of God is blessing them. Press home the truth more earnestly than ever when the Lord is opening ears and hearts to accept it. You will soon know when there is dew about, prize the gracious visitation. The farmer says, 'Make hay while the sun shines.' You cannot make the sun shine; that is quite out of your power; but you can use the sun while he shines. 'When thou hearest the sound of a going in the tops of the mulberry trees, then thou shalt bestir thyself.'[3] Be diligent in season and out of season; but in a lively season be doubly laborious.

Evermore, in beginning, in continuing, and in ending any and every good work, *consciously and in very truth depend upon the Holy Ghost*. Even a sense of your need of Him He must give you; and the prayers with which you entreat Him to come must come from Him. You are engaged in a work so spiritual, so far above all human power, that to forget

---

3.    2 Samuel 5:24.

the Spirit is to ensure defeat. Make the Holy Ghost to be the *sine qua non* of your efforts, and go so far as to say to Him, 'If Thy presence go not with us, carry us not up hence.' Rest only in Him and then *reserve for Him all the glory.* Be specially mindful of this, for this is a tender point with Him: He will not give His glory to another. Take care to praise the Spirit of God from your inmost heart, and gratefully wonder that He should condescend to work by you. Please Him by glorifying Christ. Render Him homage by yielding yourself to His impulses, and by hating everything that grieves Him. The consecration of your whole being will be the best psalm in His praise.

There are a few things which I would have you remember, and then I have done. Remember that the Holy Spirit has His ways and methods, and there are some things which He will not do. Bethink you that *He makes no promise to bless compromises.* If we make a treaty with error or sin, we do it at our own risk. If we do anything that we are not clear about, if we tamper with truth or holiness, if we are friends of the world, if we make provision for the flesh, if we preach half-heartedly and are in league with errorists, we have no promise that the Holy Spirit will go with us. The great promise runs in quite another strain: 'Come ye out from among them, and be ye separate, saith the Lord, and touch not the unclean thing; and I will receive you, and will be a Father unto you, and ye shall be my sons and daughters, saith the Lord God Almighty.'[4] In the New Testament only in that one place, with the exception of the Book of Revelation, is God called by the name of 'the Lord God Almighty.' If you want to know what great things the Lord can do, as the Lord God Almighty, be separate from the world, and from those who apostatize from the truth. The title, 'Lord God Almighty' is evidently quoted from the Old Testament. 'El-Shaddai', God all-sufficient, the many-breasted God. We shall never know the utmost power of God for supplying all our needs till we have cut connection once for all with everything which is not according to His mind. That was grand of Abraham when he said to the king of Sodom, 'I will not take of thee,'—a Babylonish garment, or a wedge of gold? No, no. He said, 'I will not take from

---

4.    2 Corinthians 6:17–18.

a thread even to a shoe latchet.'[5] That was 'the cut direct.' The man of God will have nothing to do with Sodom, or with false doctrine. If you see anything that is evil, give it the cut direct. Have done with those who have done with truth. Then you will be prepared to receive the promise, and not till then.

Dear brethren, remember that wherever there is great love, there is sure to be great jealousy. 'Love is strong as death.' What next? 'Jealousy is cruel as the grave.' 'God is love'; and for that very reason 'The Lord thy God is a jealous God.'[6] Keep clear of everything that defiles, or that would grieve the Holy Spirit; for if He be vexed with us, we shall soon be put to shame before the enemy.

Note, next, that *He makes no promise to cowardice.* If you allow the fear of man to rule you, and wish to save self from suffering or ridicule, you will find small comfort in the promise of God. 'He that saveth his life shall lose it.' The promises of the Holy Spirit to us in our warfare are to those who quit themselves like men, and by faith are made brave in the hour of conflict. I wish that we were come

---

5.    Genesis 14:23.
6.    Song of Solomon 8:6.

to this pass, that we utterly despised ridicule and calumny. Oh, to have the self-oblivion of that Italian martyr of whom Foxe speaks! They condemned him to be burned alive, and he heard the sentence calmly. But, you know, burning martyrs, however delightful, is also expensive; and the mayor of the town did not care to pay for the faggots[7], and the priests who had accused him also wished to do the work without personal expense. So they had an angry squabble, and there stood the poor man for whose benefits these faggots were to be contributed, quietly hearing their mutual recriminations. Finding that they could not settle it, he said: 'Gentlemen, I will end your dispute. It is a pity that you should, either of you, be at so much expense to find faggots for my burning, and, for my Lord's sake, I will even pay for the wood that burns me, if you please.' There is a fine touch of scorn as well as meekness there. I do not know that I would have paid that bill; but I have even felt inclined to go a little out of the way to help the enemies of the truth to find fuel for their criticisms of me. Yes, yes; I will yet be more vile, and give them more to complain

---

7.    a bundle of sticks used to start a fire.

of. I will go through with the controversy for Christ's sake, and do nothing whatever to quiet their wrath. Brethren, if you trim a little, if you try to save a little of your repute with the men of the apostasy, it will go ill with you. He that is ashamed of Christ and His Word in this evil generation shall find that Christ is ashamed of him at the last.

I will be very brief on these points. Remember, next, that *the Holy Ghost will never set His seal to falsehood.* Never! If what you preach is not the truth, God will not own it. See ye well to this.

What is more, *the Holy Ghost never sets His signature to a blank.* That would be unwise on the part of man, and the holy Lord will not perpetrate such a folly. If we do not speak clear doctrine with plainness of speech, the Holy Ghost will not put His signature to our empty prating. If we do not come out distinctly with Christ and Him crucified, we may say farewell to true success.

Next, remember that *the Holy Ghost will never sanction sin;* and to bless the ministry of some men would be to sanction their evil ways. 'Be ye clean, that bear the vessels of the Lord.'[8] Let

8.    Isaiah 52:11.

your character correspond with your teaching, and let your churches be purged from open transgressors, lest the Holy Ghost disown your teaching, not for its own sake, but because of the ill savour of unholy living which dishonours it.

Remember, again, that *He will never encourage idleness.* The Holy Ghost will not come to rescue us from the consequences of wilful neglect of the Word of God and study. If we allow ourselves to go up and down all the week doing nothing, we may not climb the pulpit stairs and dream that the Lord will be there and then tell us what to speak. If help were promised to such, then the lazier the man the better the sermon. If the Holy Spirit worked only by impromptu speakers, the less we read our Bibles and the less we meditated on them the better. If it be wrong to quote from books, 'attention to reading' should not have been commanded. All this is obviously absurd, and not one of you will fall into such a delusion. We are bound to be much in meditation, and give ourselves wholly to the Word of God and prayer, and when we have minded these things we may look for the Spirit's approbation and co-operation. We ought to prepare the sermon

as if all depended upon us, and then we are
to trust the Spirit of God knowing that all
depends upon Him. The Holy Ghost sends
no one into the harvest to sleep among the
sheaves, but to bear the burden and heat
of the day. We may well pray God to send
more *'labourers'* into the vineyard; for the
Spirit will be with the strength of labourers,
but He will not be the friend of loiterers.

Recollect, again, that *the Holy Ghost will
not bless us in order to sustain our pride.* Is it
not possible that we may be wishing for
a great blessing that we may be thought
great men? This will hinder our success:
the string of the bow is out of order and
the arrow will turn aside. What does God
do with men that are proud? Does He exalt
them? I trow not. Herod made an eloquent
oration, and he put on a dazzling silver robe
which glistened in the sun, and when the
people saw his vestments and listened to his
charming voice, they cried, 'It is the voice of
a god, and not of a man'; but the Lord smote
him, and he was eaten of worms.[9] Worms
have a prescriptive right to proud flesh; and
when we get very mighty and very big, the

---

9.    Acts 12:22.

worms expect to make a meal of us. 'Pride goeth before destruction, and a haughty spirit before a fall.'[10] Keep humble if you would have the Spirit of God with you. The Holy Ghost takes no pleasure in the inflated oratory of the proud; how can He? Would you have Him sanction bombast? 'Walk humbly with thy God', O preacher! for thou canst not walk with Him in any other fashion; and if thou walk not with Him, thy walking will be vain.

Consider, again, that *the Holy Ghost will not dwell where there is strife*. Let us follow peace with all men, and specially let us keep peace in our churches. Some of you are not yet favoured with this boon; and possibly it is not your fault. You have inherited old feuds. In many a small community, all the members of the congregation are cousins to one another, and relations usually agree to disagree. When cousins cozen their cousins, the seeds of ill-will are sown, and these intrude even into church life. Your predecessor's high-handedness in past time may breed a good deal of quarrelling for many years to come. He was a man of war from his youth, and even when he is gone the

10.  Proverbs 16:18.

spirits which he called from the vasty deep remain to haunt the spot. I fear you cannot expect much blessing, for the Holy Dove does not dwell by troubled waters: He chooses to come where brotherly love continues. For great principles, and matters of holy discipline, we may risk peace itself; but for self or party may such conduct be far from us.

Lastly, remember *the Holy Ghost will only bless in conformity with His own set purpose.* Our Lord explains what that purpose is: 'He shall glorify me.'[11] He has come forth for this grand end, and He will not put up with anything short of it. If, then, we do not preach Christ, what is the Holy Ghost to do with our preaching? If we do not make the Lord Jesus glorious; if we do not lift Him high in the esteem of men, if we do not labour to make Him King of kings, and Lord of lords; we shall not have the Holy Spirit with us. Vain will be rhetoric, music, architecture, energy, and social status: if our one design be not to magnify the Lord Jesus, we shall work alone and work in vain.

This is all I have to say to you at this time; but, my dear brethren, it is a great all if first

---

11. John 16:14.

considered, and then carried out. May it have practical effect upon us! It will, if the great Worker uses it, and not else. Go forth, O soldiers of Jesus, with 'the sword of the Spirit, which is the word of God.' Go forth with the companies of the godly whom you lead, and let every man be strong in the Lord, and in the power of His might. As men alive from the dead, go forth in the quickening power of the Holy Ghost: you have no other strength. May the blessing of the Triune God rest upon you, one and all, for the Lord Jesus Christ's sake! Amen.